The Gospel Reloaded takes readers to the other end of the "rabbit hole."

—CRAIG DETWEILER, screenwriter, *Extreme Days*

As storyteller and innovator, pastor and prophet, Chris knows the power and beauty of culture, yet calls us to a life that transcends—a life outside the matrix. Unafraid of the intersection of the ancient text of Scripture and the modern text of film, he exposes our desperate need for God.

—CLYDE TABER, cofounder and president, Damah Film Festival: Spiritual Experiences in Film

Many choose to ignore the output of pop culture, thinking it has nothing to teach them, and that if they ignore it long enough it will simply go away. Chris Seay always disagrees—managing to find the good, analyze the bad, and teach us unexpected lessons.

—MARK JOSEPH, author, *Faith, God & Rock 'n' Roll*

Instead of throwing rocks at culture and Hollywood, Chris Seay and Greg Garrett seek to build bridges. This is simply the best book on the deeper meaning of *The Matrix*.

—DAVID BRUCE, web master, HollywoodJesus.com

THE GOSPEL
RELOADED

EXPLORING SPIRITUALITY
AND FAITH IN *the Matrix*

CHRIS SEAY
AND GREG GARRETT

PIÑON PRESS ®

OUR GUARANTEE TO YOU

Piñon Press
P.O. Box 35007
Colorado Springs, CO 80935

© 2003 by James Christopher Seay

ISBN 1-57683-478-6

Cover design: The Office of Bill Chiaravalle, www.officeofbc.com
            Benjamin Kinzer
Creative Team: Jay Howver, Steve Halliday, Greg Clouse, Darla Hightower, Pat Miller

CIP Data Applied For

Printed in the United States of America

2 3 4 5 6 7 8 9 10/ 07 06 05 04 03

_ C O N T E N T S _

ACKNOWLEDGMENTS

CHRIS:

For Lisa (my beautiful bride), Hanna (my five-year-old princess explorer), Trinity (my beautiful two-year-old), and my son Solomon: You all make my life sweet.

To Mom, Dad, Brian, Amy, Jen, Rusty, Robbie, Liz, Jessica, Noni, Papa, Terry, Sharon, Lisa, Eddie, Sam, Ruth, Sammy, Hannah, Pam, and Bob: Thank you for the important part you play in our life!

To my friend, Greg, whose skill and friendship make this process a joy.

To Ecclesia and the elders (Chad, Robbie, Justin, Paul, and Tim) and staff (Tyndall, Christy, Jennifer, Tom, and Steve), for being the kind of community that inspires and encourages this kind of reflection and creation.

To everyone at Piñon Press, for doing your jobs so well. It is a pleasure working with all of you. Special thanks to Kent, Dan, Jay, Jennifer, Sarah, Terry, Amy, Lisa, Kathleen, Nicci, Toben, Greg, Darla, Mike, and certainly not least the hard-working, culturally adept sales team.

To Eugene Peterson for *The Message*: You have given us a beautiful gift.

To Steve Halliday, my editor and new friend: Thank you.

To West End Baptist Church, Emergent, Youth Specialties, Baylor University/Art & Soul, Houston Astros, our friends at the *Houstonian* (especially those that play with our children in the Bungalow, make great food at Center Court, and Johnny, George, Clement, and Wayland for the great smoothies).

To the best restaurants in Houston where much of this book was written: Arcodoro, Tia Maria's, Cavatore, La Tour D' Argent, Todai, Café Adobe, Papasitos, Doyles, 9 Amigo's at Minute Maid Park, Collina's, Mai's, and Barnaby's.

GREG:

For Jake, who loves the movies, and with thanks to my buddy Chris, who makes writing fun.

To Seventh & James Baptist Church, St. James Episcopal Church, Scott Walker, Tom Hanks, the Austin Public Library, and all the good people at Piñon Press.

And to those at Baylor University: Dean Wallace Daniel and the Arts & Sciences Sabbatical Committee, Provost David Lyle Jeffrey, Bob Darden, and my students in the Spring 2003 Art of Film class, especially Alex Adler, Hans Christianson, Smith Getterman, Michelle Holland, Mike Schudel, Alathea Sloan, and Trent Terrell.

_ I N T R O D U C T I O N _

On Easter weekend, 1999, moviegoers first entered *The Matrix*. They came for the adventure, the martial arts, the gritty vision of a bleak science fiction future. Or they came to see Keanu Reeves and Laurence Fishburne. They *all* left blown away by the story, by the ideas — and, of course, by amazing images they had never before seen on film.

The Matrix reached large audiences in the nation's cineplexes, but it really took hold upon its entry into the world of home video. The format's digital sound and video capabilities — combined with its offer of additional information about a movie and its ideas — made *The Matrix* the first breakout hit on DVD. Even four years later, in early 2003, it remained one of the hundred best-selling DVDs on Amazon.com.

Yet perhaps most important to the film's success is the richness and density of its story, ideas, and images. The writers/directors, brothers Larry and Andy Wachowski, began a spiritual dialogue and articulated the story of faith in ways no one had expected. For that reason alone, *The Matrix* truly is a film worthy of multiple viewings, considerations, and conversations.

In a world searching for common ground and a basis for peace, *The Matrix* provides a point of intersection where all of our stories collide: Buddhism meets Christianity and Homer's *Odyssey* meets the childhood epic *Alice in Wonderland*. In this film they not only coexist, they come together to create a story of tension, adventure, and spiritual pursuit. As Buddhism, Christianity, Zen, existentialism, Gnosticism, Plato, and Jacques Derrida interact with one another, we are encouraged to interact with them as well.

The many myths, stories, and ideas that appear in the film seem obvious even to the most casual viewers. Richard Corliss, writing in *Time* magazine, first spotted the movie references: science fiction dystopias like *Blade Runner* and *The Terminator*, Hong Kong action films (both martial arts and John Woo gunplay), Japanese anime. But Corliss noted that the Wachowski brothers seem to have a larger scope in mind; they "want to meld classic lit, hallucinogenic imagery, and a wild world of philosophical surmises to pop culture. The Bible meets Batman; Lewis Carroll collides with William Gibson; Greek and geek mythology bump and run."[1] It is a film dense with metaphor and meaning and allegorical levels, but at the same time it delivers the action and excitement that draws mass audiences.

Larry Wachowski told *Time*, "We wrote the story for ourselves and hoped others would pick up on it. . . . Every studio we showed it to thought no one would understand it. We told them it would be complex and dense, but we were also going to shoot the best action scenes and the coolest computer graphics ever. Even if audiences didn't get all of the references, we knew they'd at least have a good time with the visuals."[2]

But a surprising number of people who had a good time with the visuals also want to examine the references, to consider the philosophy behind the film, to talk about the correspondences between the world and situation of the movie's main character, Neo/Thomas Anderson

(Keanu Reeves), and our own. They watch the movie repeatedly; they contribute threads to online discussion boards and create more than a thousand websites about the film; they talk about *The Matrix* in coffee-houses; they explore it in church.

That the movie offers so many layers and levels of meaning does not perplex this audience. It transfixes them as it does us, the authors of this book. To us, *The Matrix* seems like a huge tapestry woven from beautiful threads, silk and silver and gold, each of which has strength and beauty, each of which we can trace from its beginnings to its end, but each of which weaves together with other threads to create a rich, complex design. *The Matrix* is a truly postmodern work in its weaving of influences and multiple realities; in this book, we will examine the threads, singly and together, to find meanings that may help us make sense of the questions in our lives.

To that end, we intend to focus on the religious and spiritual values in the film. While the Wachowskis remain notably reclusive and have said very little about their film, preferring for audiences to find their own meanings, they have acknowledged their interest in the metaphysical in web chats and in print. According to Larry Wachowski, "We are interested in mythology, theology, and to a lesser extent, higher-level mathematics. . . . All are ways human beings try to answer bigger questions, as well as The Big Question. If you're going to do epic stories, you should concern yourself with those issues. . . . We wanted to make people think, engage their minds a bit."[3]

Likewise, we hope to engage your mind, to talk about why we think a great adventure movie can also teach us about faith and hope and other religious issues. Both of us have used the film as a spiritual touchstone—Chris in talks and sermons, Greg in the university classroom—but this megastory has reached a far wider religious audience than churches and schools. A reviewer in *Christianity Today* picked it as one of 1999's best films; a writer in *Books and Culture* defended the film against charges of excessive violence; stories at beliefnet.com have traced the correspondences between Neo and Jesus Christ; and the *Journal of Religion and Film* already has published several significant scholarly articles on *The Matrix*.

And interest shows no sign of slowing; rather, with the film's two sequels, a video game, and a series of computer-animated short films appearing in short order, a *Newsweek* cover recently called 2003 "The Year of *The Matrix*."

The Matrix and its interrelated stories tell us about fate and free will, alienation and chosen-ness, ontology and nothingness, authority and revolution, justice and mercy, playacting and authentic living. *The Matrix* insists that we are part of a larger living story, that miracles can happen, that individuals can play a part in their own redemption, that death is not the end. Follow us down the rabbit hole, through the mirror, and see what else the movie has to say.

_ 1 //

_ E X P E R I E N C E   T H E   M A T R I X _

Prophesy, interpretate the signs. Nothing is really what it seems.

P. O. D. , *Sonny Sandoval*

I must acknowledge the awkward dissonance that comes in writing a book about *The Matrix*. On every level it is a story that we must experience. The visuals stun you; the music startles and sometimes disturbs. Taken together, the elements have the power to stir viewers into a film-induced frenzy.

As Neo demonstrated his newfound gift for kung fu in the first *Matrix* film, I wanted to try out the same moves on the obnoxious popcorn smacker behind me. Time and space seemed completely irrelevant as the overpowering phenomenon that was *The Matrix* consumed me. I lost myself in the experience.

So it is with tremendous sensitivity that we reflect on that experience in this book. I believe that reflecting on our common experience through the *Matrix* films is not only appropriate, but essential. Morpheus is right: "No one can be told what the matrix is—you must see it for yourself."

I'm assuming that no one would read this book who has not already viewed these films and somehow been affected by them. Richard Corliss has described the effects of the first film in *Time* magazine: "*The Matrix* stoked the adrenaline of millions of moviegoers and the intellects of many active, lonely minds."[1] These motion pictures create a number of reactions in viewers, and while their creators didn't make them for the sole purpose of giving instruction about faith and philosophy, that's what happens nonetheless.

THE THIRST TO UNDERSTAND

In a song written for the *The Matrix: Reloaded* soundtrack, P.O.D., the famed MTV rock band, echoes the sentiments of millions of *Matrix* fans searching for meaning through the movie—and in their lives:

> Reveal to me the mysteries
> Can you tell me what it means?
> Explain these motions and metaphors
> Unlock these secrets in me
> Describe your vision, the meaning is missing
> Won't anybody listen?[2]

P.O.D. front man Sonny Sandoval said of his band's involvement in the film, "This movie has a lot of biblical themes, and so [the directors] wanted to keep that vibe. I got the concept [for "Sleeping Awake"] from Daniel interpreting King Nebuchadnezzar's dreams in the Old Testament."[3]

The mysteries of *The Matrix* seem almost as elusive as the dreams of this ancient king. This book is an attempt to guide us in the journey—not merely as an expedition to figure out *The Matrix*, but to seek our own enlightenment. If movie theaters have become the new cathedrals, as cultural observers from Bill Moyers to George Lucas argue, then the priests of that domain are clad in black leather. And Cool Hand Luke, Obi-Wan Kenobi, and E.T. assist in serving the sacrament.

KNOWLEDGE DOESN'T SAVE

As Morpheus guides Neo and other seekers of truth, he encourages them simply to walk the path. The immature often assume they find the road to development in knowledge. When Neo ponders the powers of the Oracle, he wonders if she knows everything. Morpheus responds, "She would say she knows enough."

So if her power does not lie in her vast intellect, then Neo assumes it must spring from her divination of truth. In that case, the words that flow from her mouth must be infallible. Again Morpheus explains: "Try not to think of it in terms of right or wrong."

The counsel of the Oracle should not be regarded as scientifically proven; it exists to help one find the path. As we will see, in the *Matrix* films the Wachowski brothers have combined action and insight, destruction and devotion. The end result powerfully encourages and even provokes us to explore what it means to walk a spiritual path.

ENLIGHTENMENT IN UNEXPECTED PLACES

So set aside your disbelief. Enlightenment comes from many sources, often unexpected.

But why hide nuggets of wisdom in an action film? Well, if the Wachowski brothers had made a documentary on the great religious and philosophical discoveries of humanity, 150 people (maybe) might have made it out to the cinemas. Instead, they crafted a film inspired by many of those concepts, added kung fu and state-of-the-art effects—and the film pulled in $460 million at the theaters (which adds up to tens of millions of viewers worldwide, plus the many millions who have since seen the film on video).

In the process, millions of viewers have come face-to-face with Big Ideas. *The Matrix* and its sequels create a space for reflection, for contemplation of crucial issues of life: faith, wisdom, and eternity. They show us dramatically what it means—how hard it can be—to recognize the path, to accept it, to walk it.

In this book, we'll ask you to enter the experience of the films. Walk the path with us. Open your heart and mind. There is a reason you have chosen to read this book.

Morpheus tells us, "There are no accidents. We have not come here by chance. I do not believe in chance."

Neither do we.

_2 //

_ W H A T   I S   T H E   M A T R I X ? _

I can visualize a time in the future
when we will be to robots as dogs are to humans.

CLAUDE SHANNON, *The Mathematical Theory of Communication*, 1949

It's the question that drives you. It causes you to doubt everything and suspect everyone around you. Nothing is what it seems; all five senses lie to you; only intuition tells the truth. It cries out on every street corner and quietly whispers through the silence: *Wake up!*

The matrix is an enigma. We know only that it either holds us forcibly or keeps us restrained by our own choosing. The only difference between us and the characters in the film is that many among us still await a call from outside, like the one that aroused Neo's curiosity: "Wake up, Neo. The matrix has you."

At times in the film I began to question the nature of my own existence. Did the matrix have me?

On the first morning of Neo's training, the crew of the *Nebuchadnezzar* reminisced about the flavor-filled food in the matrix and lamented their bland amino-protein compound. But in reality, the tastes they remember may be an error in the matrix; maybe that is why almost everything tastes like chicken.

The argument sounded so compelling that I began to lose myself in the story. This is the power of the *Matrix* films. At no time during *Star Wars* did I ever consider the possibility that the story might actually be true. *The Matrix* represents the most effective kind of science fiction— complete fantasy that seems like reality.

Since we ultimately agree that the films are fiction and that the concept of the matrix symbolizes something much larger, however, let us consider a few possible interpretations.

THE MATRIX AS MODERNITY

According to the dictionary, the word *matrix* comes from the Latin meaning "womb." It gives form, origin, or foundation to something enclosed or embedded within another thing.

The film captures a window in time at the end of the twentieth century in which civilization began to give birth to something new. Modernity had reigned supreme for five hundred years, but the old girl finally ran out of gas. And what would replace her, this era that elevated science and reason above all? Who knows?

Some hope that postmodernity will bring out the best of the modern age: the pursuit of knowledge, medical and technological advancement, and the ability of human beings to become increasingly interconnected, despite the barrier of individualism. And perhaps it will be so. If we can abandon the arrogance that led to modernity's downfall, we might find a recipe for success—if we choose to *value* science instead of *worshiping* it.

The quest of modern man (and his patriarch, René Descartes) to "master the natural realm" is, at best, presumptive. When teamed with a flawed view of progress that considers mankind and civilization as getting inevitably better, the quest reveals itself as flat-out ludicrous. The more we learn, the more we realize how much more we have to learn. Even as economic theories grow increasingly advanced and stock markets make use of ever-more-sophisticated computer trading systems, still we cannot seem to feed the starving millions of the Third World or effectively treat the crisis of AIDS that ravages the continent at the center of our own world.

So in some ways, *The Matrix* embodies our darkest moment in history. Consider it an everlasting Polaroid of "the peak of our civilization," as Agent Smith said mockingly. Descartes spoke of the ability of an evil deceiver who might use dreams to betray humanity—and ironically, modern dreams reflect the world that Descartes midwifed into existence. In the case of the film, a mighty artificial intelligence attempts to lull mankind back into the false security of modernity, namely, the belief that they remain in control.

Do *you* believe that you control your own fate? If so, maybe the matrix has you, too.

The Matrix as Organized Religion

My coauthor, Greg, has a student who declared that the matrix resembles nothing so much as organized religion and our involvement with it. This student saw the two as similar systems that keep people asleep, dreaming and docile, unable to ask questions or imagine alternatives.

Many Gen-X and Gen-Yers share this jaundiced view, and thus share much in common with Neo. When Bill Stamets pointed out in his *Chicago Reader* review of the film that "a few angst-ridden souls like Neo sense that the world is awry, but the vast majority don't have a clue. Our minds live in the Matrix . . . where we dream our lives, eyes shut in a collective hallucination,"[1] he also described the experience of many of the film's viewers. Greg's student just happens to be a particularly literate example, as you'll see from the following:

> I would equate organized religion with the matrix: a system
> firmly in place that gives us an acceptable way to deal with
> reality and gives us a plausible way to answer the unanswerable
> questions. A way to substantiate and cope with death. A way
> to relinquish control and not worry about the things we can't
> control. Religion, in my mind, is a system that allows you to
> exist in the world and not think. An elaborate system of tradi-
> tions and procedures to follow that guarantees, in our minds,
> an acceptable avenue to the afterlife of our choice. And obvi-
> ously, religious traditions vary greatly. I see this as the fact that
> "you are how you see yourself" in the matrix, and that you
> are in a sense responsible for creating your own reality with
> the available resources.
>
> There have been many frustrated moments in my life
> when I've looked at what I, at that point in time, felt was a
> bumbling, moronic populace. It disgusted me that they could
> so simply find solace and affirmation in such a far-fetched
> social construct as God. It's there, they accept it, they don't
> question it, because to question it would mean facing some
> really difficult issues and doubts, so they just go with the
> flow. "God is in control"—so I don't have to be. Freud called

religion nothing more than a defense mechanism. (I don't always feel this way — I don't want to come off as blatantly atheistic or anything, but I've had the doubt myself.)

In *The Matrix*, the defense mechanism has advanced to such a degree — it is so firmly held in place — that society isn't even aware of it. People aren't allowed to pursue it; it's just there, enslaving them all. Think of the Agents as the people who come down on you every time you try to examine thoughts independent of the religion that has been so firmly implanted in your life. They squelch doubt, not by encouraging you to pursue your own thoughts and arrive at your own conclusions, but instead by sticking a metaphorical gun in your face and threatening you with non-acceptance and the threat that you will go to hell if you don't conform.

So if organized religion is the matrix and the devout members of our society who can't tolerate thought independent of religious principles (or who scoff at religious questions as if they were sin) are the Agents — then who are the good guys? Who is Morpheus? Who is Neo? Who are the people who realize that the matrix is just an illusion designed to pacify society, a system constructed to keep them from realizing what's really going on? Are they atheists? Reckless rebels who challenge the way things work and who thus pose a threat to normal existence? Agent Smith refers to Morpheus as the most dangerous man in the world. But why?

Is it because they advance new ideas? Is it because they threaten the sanctity of the illusion? Of course. In our world, people who challenge mainstream thought regularly get turned into villains. And this doesn't just have to be religious issues; they can be social, political, anything outside the mainstream. Just look at Galileo. People don't ultimately care about what's real, about truth. They care only about what's accepted. Galileo was banished and excommunicated and put under house arrest—yet he was *right*. He was punished for daring to make an observation that pointed out a fallacy in the way society looked at itself. For altering definitions.

In the movie, Morpheus tells us to challenge everything we've been taught, to abandon all our beliefs, to accept that reality as we see it isn't real. And he has sought out Neo—the One, Jesus, if you will—to lead the crusade and save enslaved mankind by showing them what is real. By challenging everything. By making them aware that they are slaves, and thus opening the doors to true redemption.[2]

THERE IS NO SPOON

What is real? How can we know? If reality is what we can feel, smell, taste, and see, then the God we worship walks outside of our understanding of reality.

People of faith are no strangers to this idea, regardless of whether they have given it serious thought. They gather in churches, mosques, and synagogues each week to worship something they believe is real, even though it cannot be physically quantified. Christ tells us of a kingdom that cannot be seen with human eyes, offers invisible water that will cure all thirst, and beckons us to participate in the world of the unseen.

Genuine faith is about living in an alternate reality—rejecting the embrace of the physical realm in exchange for a higher plane. The trick, of course, is that the physical world desires our complete attention, and it seduces us with things we can own: cars, homes, televisions, technology, and emblems of status.

Paradoxically, people of faith want the physical realm to prove their belief in the unseen. Even among the most faithful, laity and clergy strive to validate their own beliefs through science and reason. Religious historians and archaeologists seek to "prove" the reality of Noah's ark or that the Shroud of Turin is truly the burial clothes of Jesus. Scientists, theologians, and philosophers promote the theory of intelligent design to "explain" the birth of our universe and the genesis of life on earth. The tension challenges us. We want to believe yet look for help from science.

We can find evidence of the supernatural on this mortal plane, but we will not discover it under a microscope or revealed in a math equation. In beauty we smell the sweet scent of the Creator and witness the nature of the divine. God is manifest through the laugh of a child. We feel his power in our awe of nature.

The matrix is an illusion, providing blinders for our eyes that hide the true reality. We do not want to see what is real; we rush past it. Atheists deny their faith in the spiritual realm and settle for the wonder of the world they inhabit, while many Christians make the opposite mistake. They hide from the culture and create a fantasy world around themselves. They love the soft, pastel world of the "painter of light," Thomas Kinkade, who creates dreamy scenes in sync with what many Christians long for. In contrast, the perplexed young filmmaker in Alan Ball's *American Beauty* turns his camera toward death—be it of an old woman or a crumpled, decaying bird—and declares it "beauty." Which artist is working from the world as it is?

We long to see the world through rose-colored glasses, but the jaded edges of life cannot be ignored forever. When we become enlightened, we, like Neo, wake up disoriented and uncomfortable in the "desert of the real." Morpheus explains: "This is the world you know, the world as it existed at the end of the twentieth century." It is a world filled with skyscrapers, computers, nightclubs, and busy streets. "You've been living in a dream world, Neo. This is the world as it exists today." The bright earth shrivels into an immense, dark tomb, scorched from soil to sky. No green interrupts the horizon—no signs of life—only ghostly shades of black. "Welcome to the desert of the real."

Carrie-Anne Moss (the actress who portrays Trinity) spoke of her comprehension of the matrix in an interview on the official *Matrix* website:

> It reminded me of one time at school when a teacher proposed this question to the class: "What if, right now, our sitting in this classroom is just a dream? What if our lives are just dreams?" And in that moment, even though we didn't have big discussions about it, a seed was planted in my mind: it was the first time I thought that maybe life is not the way I was told and taught, maybe things are different. You grow up believing in evolution or religion or that the world is flat, and whatever you've been told is what you believe. I thought that day it could be something different, something I'm not aware of. Sometimes I'll be walking through life and I'll go, "Am I dreaming? How do I know this isn't a dream?" That's kind of *The Matrix*.

WHO IS RIGHT?

What do the Wachowski brothers say about the true nature of the matrix? What do they claim it is? They don't say—and therein lies the point. The film's official website (www.whatisthematrix.com) highlights their reluctance to say.

The question is more important than the answer. Or more importantly, asking ourselves the question(s) is more significant than our accepting without question an answer—any answer. What holds us back, restrains our ambition, and silences our potential? The unthinking, unreasoning, unquestioning acceptance of anything.

But we can allow the journey of *The Matrix* to serve as our wake-up call. Divine moments come and beckon us to follow our own white rabbits. We must risk losing our safety in order to see things more clearly. Then we will see the true nature of the matrix: a crutch, whether it be modern arrogance, mindless religion, or simply dim vision.

_ 3 //

_ P O S T M O D E R N   S T E W _

One of our crises, as we enter the postmodern world, is that Christianity has presented itself as a system of belief instead of a story.

B R I A N   M c L A R E N

Early in his essay on *The Matrix*, *Time* magazine's Richard Corliss described the first appearance of Laurence Fishburne as the character Morpheus: "a morphing Orpheus, a black White Rabbit, an R-and-B Obi-Wan Kenobi, a big bad John the Baptist, a Gandalf who grooves; every wise guide from literature, religion, movies, and comics."[1] Corliss, like most others who saw the film, got the point: *The Matrix* combines styles and stories in a perfect postmodern mishmash of narrative and symbol. They are too numerous to name, and yet following many of these threads back to their sources gives us a greater understanding of this film and the reasons we feel drawn to it.

Out of those tangled threads, audiences can pick and choose, can follow or leave alone, because the important thing is that at least one story will hit a viewer where he or she thinks and lives. The others may connect on a second viewing. Over time, the Wachowski brothers take all of their potent narratives and learned influences and make them accessible to mass audiences in the format of a feature film trilogy.

To get the most out of the movies—and to understand the most of their thoughtful and playful appropriation of story lines and belief systems—one ought to assess the influences on the Wachowski brothers as they wrote their screenplays. In this chapter, we'll examine the literary, religious, cinematic, and comic book predecessors of Neo, Morpheus, Trinity, and others and begin to pursue the meanings of *The Matrix*.

THE HERO'S JOURNEY

The Matrix draws heavily from the archetypal myth of the hero that we see in almost every story of importance, from *The Epic of Gilgamesh* (the first written work of literature, from Sumeria) to Moses to Jesus to the latest edition of the *Star Wars* saga. Scholar Joseph Campbell crystallized our understanding of this universal myth in his classic work of cultural anthropology, *The Hero with a Thousand Faces*. Campbell discovered that virtually every great story—whether myth, religion, or literature—conforms to a similar pattern:

> The usual hero adventure begins with someone from whom something has been taken, or who feels there is something lacking in the normal experiences available or permitted to the members of his society. The person then takes off on a series of adventures beyond the ordinary, either to recover what has been lost or to discover some life-giving elixir. It's usually a cycle, a coming and a returning.[2]

Campbell found in all of these myths—and in the rhythms, flows, ceremonies, and milestones of our own lives—an archetypal pattern that has brought meaning to people for three thousand years. This pattern provides the structure of *The Matrix* as well.

Thomas Anderson/Neo lives in the mundane Ordinary World which will be revealed to him as the matrix, but which to us looks all too familiar: the world of work, play, activity, and emptiness. Neo receives the Call to Adventure when Trinity and Morpheus unexpectedly contact him. When he refuses to climb around the ledge onto the scaffolding to escape the Agents for the first time, he refuses the Call to escape into another world—at least for the time being. But after his release, Neo meets his mentor, Morpheus, face-to-face, and Morpheus makes the Call to Adventure specific in two colored capsules: if Neo takes the blue capsule, he will wake up in his bed, back in the Ordinary World of the matrix. But if he takes the red capsule, "You stay in Wonderland and I show you how deep the rabbit hole goes."

When Neo takes the red capsule and allows the crew of the *Nebuchadnezzar* to home in on his actual body, he crosses the First Threshold. By agreeing to leave the Ordinary World, Neo "agrees to face the consequences of dealing with the problem or challenge posed in the Call to Adventure."[3] Once he crosses the Threshold, the second act of the story begins: Neo faces tests and meets both allies and enemies. He must learn the truth about his existence in the matrix, test his skills against Morpheus and the jump program (where he fails his first leap of faith), contend with Cypher's temptations to disbelieve, and enter the matrix to consult the Oracle. The crew's escape, despite Cypher's betrayal and Morpheus' capture, prompt the end of this act: the Approach to the Inmost Cave and the Ordeal.

When Neo (with Trinity) chooses to return to the matrix to confront the Agents and rescue Morpheus, he descends into the bowels of hell, crossing a second major Threshold. In the battle that secures the lobby of the building—and the battle on the roof that follows—Neo infiltrates the place of greatest possible danger, the stronghold of his enemies. The

Ordeal that follows—when he puts the Agents at the business end of a machine gun and when he rescues Morpheus and Trinity by exhibiting superhuman strength and agility—brings Neo close to death. The Oracle has told him he is not the One, but by choosing to act as if he is, Neo saves his friends—and moves closer to the ultimate Reward.

The Reward, for Neo and the others, is the knowledge that he is (or at least, may be) the One. But how to reconcile this with the Oracle's words: "Maybe in your next life"? On The Road Back, Neo and the others must find an exit; allowing Morpheus and Trinity to go before him, he is unknowingly left alone with Agent Smith. Here, for the first time, a human faces an Agent with something like a chance of victory. In the fight that follows, Neo claims his heritage—again, affirming the Reward—when he says, "I am Neo," just before his temporary defeat of Agent Smith. But there is yet another step in the hero's journey before he can return to the ship: Resurrection. As story consultant Christopher Vogler explains it:

> This is often a second life-and-death moment. . . . Death and
> darkness get in one last desperate shot before being finally
> defeated. It's kind of a final exam for the hero, who must be
> tested once more to see if he has really learned the lessons of
> the Ordeal.[4]

Neo gets shot and killed by Agent Smith. He slumps to the floor as aboard the *Nebuchadnezzar* the sentinels prepare to destroy the ship and its crew. But Trinity brings Neo back—in the best fairy tale tradition, with a kiss, and in the best philosophical tradition, with an argument: he can't be dead, because the Oracle told her the man she fell in love with would be the One. She loves Neo; therefore, Neo is the One; therefore, Neo cannot be dead. And he isn't. Instead he transforms into a new creature, a true hero, and can now return with new insight and power.

The Matrix more implies than shows his Return with the Elixir. Neo returns to his body and kisses Trinity. The implications of the Return come through the final scene, when Neo speaks into the payphone of a better world to come, a world that he wants to help bring into existence. When he flies like Superman out of the picture, we know that Neo has brought back the Elixir of his knowledge to serve society (and that we can look forward to some great sequels). *Reloaded* and *Revolutions* show us the working out of Neo's Return.

In the film's use of important hero's journeys, we see echoes of *The Odyssey*, Moses and the Exodus, the life of Gautama Buddha, the life of Christ, and many other sources of literature, religion, and popular culture. The Wachowski brothers dropped out of good colleges (Larry attended Bard College; Andy studied at Emerson) and both have a voracious intelligence. Their interests range from the comics to the cosmic, from cyberpunk to string theory.

It shows.

I AM . . . SUPERMAN

First, the comics. Many viewers have fallen in love with how the film so expertly creates a world familiar to comics aficionados, an atmospheric cosmos of superheroic feats, larger-than-life villains, and portentious battles between good and evil. It's not surprising, when we discover that the Wachowskis wrote comics before they came to Hollywood.

Laurence Fishburne has said that the two sequels will make the comic correspondence even stronger: "Basically, Neo becomes Superman and Morpheus becomes Batman."[5] You don't even have to be a comics reader to get the gist of his comment, for both of these characters have entered the American psyche through popular films and culture references. Batman, a black-suited creature of the night, seeks justice as a superbly trained and equipped human—like Morpheus—but a human nonetheless. He tries to save the world through his human works. He is the Old Testament.

Superman gives us a clear Messiah figure, sent to earth by a heavenly Father to save the world. He fights for truth, justice, and the American Way (back when the American Way seemed always to coincide with truth and justice). He doesn't have to follow human rules; his strength is phenomenal, his powers unearthly. You know him: "Stronger than a locomotive. . . . " Like Superman, Neo's power of flight makes him even more godlike, a hero who faces down problems that mere humans can't solve, and *Reloaded* makes the comparison explicit, talking about Neo and his "Superman thing." Superman is the New Testament.

The Matrix films owe more to comics than just some general configurations of their heroes. In the use of a dystopian society bedeviled by a deep-seated conspiracy, the films resemble many significant comics. Alan Moore's *Watchmen* deals with a world that doesn't seem to need—or want—heroes and explores what the role of hero might be in such a society. Frank Miller's *Dark Knight* series, one of the most popular in comics history, deals with the impact of superheroes on the earth—some of whom, like Batman, operate as agents of anarchy, while others, like Superman, work as agents (Agents?) behind the scenes, propping up society. *The Matrix* echoes storylines in the popular *X-Men* comic books, dealing with futures where powerful mechanical Sentinels have eradicated all mutant life and made the earth a wasteland.

Other comparisons come easily to mind. The Punisher was one of the first of a string of vigilante characters in the comics, who dressed in black, sported high-tech weaponry, and had no compunctions about killing "evil-doers." A look at both comic and film reveals many visual similarities. And *The Matrix* appeared at about the same time that a series called *The Authority* redefined superhero comics with ultra-cool heroes who refused to deal merely with the symptoms of cultural woes, but instead began to fight the root causes of injustice and terror.

The Matrix found another strong influence in Japanese manga—ultra-violent comics featuring superheroes and martial arts—and its cinematic equivalent, anime. Japanese anime has become familiar to American mainstream audiences through airings of shows like *Cowboy Bebop* on the Cartoon Network and the success of movies like *Princess Mononoke*. As those who have seen anime know, it differs from the animation that we recognize in the West; it doesn't seem to have much in common with Warner Brothers cartoons or Disney feature films. Gloria Goodale points out, "Anime generally has complex storylines, with detailed characters who routinely discuss life-and-death matters such as religion and the afterlife. The figures are usually drawn with oversize eyes reflecting the Japanese belief that the eyes are the windows of the soul."[6] (This may explain Cypher's cryptic comment to Trinity about Neo's "big, pretty eyes.")

The anime films most influential on the Wachowski brothers were the classics *Akira* (1987) and *Ghost in the Shell* (1995). Both films intersperse frenetic action scenes with philosophical reflection and depict a reality populated by machines, people, and superhumans (whether psychics or cyborgs). Likewise, they share a similar visual look, show the influence of cyberpunk, and feature tough guys (and girls) in sunglasses.

The choice of a red or blue pill in *The Matrix* seems like a nod to the prominence of pills in *Akira* and to the jacket emblem of the biker gang "The Capsules." A speech by the authority figure, the Colonel ("This city is a garbage heap."), seems to echo the speech by Agent Smith when he gets alone with Morpheus ("I hate this place. This zoo. This prison."). The staging of action scenes (including the bowing and blowing out of windows, similar to what happens in *The Matrix* when the helicopter crashes into the side of the building) also suggests that *Akira* helped to inspire portions of *The Matrix*.

But *Ghost in the Shell* appears to have exerted the most influence on the Wachowski brothers, because it shares both a similar structure and several visual elements with *The Matrix*. Both films begin with strings of green data; both employ major characters that interface with machines through plugs in the backs of their heads. The characters have a similar visual look—leather and vinyl, dark sunglasses. But perhaps more importantly, both films spend far more time discussing the nature of reality than they do in shooting lead. The main characters in *Ghost in the Shell* discourse at length on existence—who has it, when it's over, what it's about—and characters in the story have implanted memories and so don't know the difference between reality and what machines have given them. Both films also share a latent spirituality: *Ghost in the Shell* takes as its title the mystery of soul or spirit incarnated in flesh (or metal), and two quotations from the apostle Paul (the famous passages on "seeing through a glass darkly" in 1 Corinthians 13) frame the story.

The Wachowskis borrowed other visual images besides the ghostly green strings of numbers and letters. The look of the gunfights and action sequences appears almost identical, while the final action sequence, featuring a running Major Kusanagi (the movie's main character) fleeing automatic weapons, gets directly quoted in the lobby scene with Neo and Trinity against the troops. A close shot on the revolving barrel of the "Gatling gun" used against Kusanagi finds a direct echo in *The Matrix*—down to the revolving barrels—when the camera moves in on Neo during the rescue of Morpheus. Clearly, the Wachowski brothers found kindred spirits in the makers of these stories.

USE THE FORCE

Other influences outside of Japanese anime helped to shape *The Matrix*. The future worlds of the *Terminator* and *Alien* films, *Blade Runner*, and other science fiction films obviously had a tremendous impact on the design and atmosphere of the film.

The movie's fight scenes show the strong influence of Hong Kong cinema. The martial arts ballet of choreographer Yuen Wo Ping had appeared, of course, in many previous films, including his own, while the slow-motion gunplay bears the stamp of John Woo films such as *The Killer*, as well as the balance between philosophical talk and violent action characteristic of those films. The character named Mifune in *Reloaded* is a nod to the samurai action films of Japanese director Akira Kurosawa, many of which starred Toshiro Mifune. The *Matrix* universe also bears some superficial resemblance to the *Star Wars* universe, which also presents a sort of pop-culture Messiah and underlying Force. George Lucas told interviewer Bill Moyers, "I see *Star Wars* as taking all the issues that religion represents and trying to distill them down into a more modern and easily accessible construct—that there is a greater mystery out there."[7]

The Wachowskis have declared their hope to accomplish something much more serious in their presentation of ideas and beliefs than what Lucas has done. Larry told Richard Corliss, "The Force is good, fun stuff. . . . I grew up on those movies. But we were hoping to do something a little more sophisticated with *The Matrix*."[8]

And of course, because the Wachowskis are literate in so many fields, the influences could be recounted indefinitely. The early rooftop scene in which Agents chase Trinity contains visual echoes of Alfred Hitchcock's *Vertigo* (which begins with a similarly framed rooftop chase); *The Matrix* also makes characteristic use of the color green, the dominant color in *Vertigo*. The movie also uses the underlying mythology (and refers to the book and film) of *The Wizard of Oz*. Beyond that, the camera angles and editing in the subway station standoff between Agent Smith and Neo evoke Western films from *Stagecoach* to *High Noon* to *Silverado*. And playing on television in the Oracle's house we see the movie *Night of the Lepus*, an obscure science fiction film about giant bunnies—a continuation of the white rabbit motif in ridiculous form. The white rabbit thread comes from Lewis Carroll's *Alice in Wonderland*, while Neo's experience with the mercury-mirror could be drawn from Carroll's sequel, *Adventures Through the Looking Glass*. The cyberpunk novels of William Gibson contribute plot and character threads, as does the cyberpunk movement itself.

The Wachowski brothers managed to weave this tapestry together and maintain a coherent story line with a premise both complicated and far-fetched. Other so-called "virtual reality films" released in the early 1990s became the dogs of Tinseltown. *Virtuosity* (starring Denzel Washington and Russell Crowe), *The Lawnmower Man*, *Arcade*, and *Ghost in the Machine* proved only that writing a screenplay to present a coherent VR story is more challenging than the Wachowskis make it look. Within months of the release of *The Matrix*, other studios took their shot at this emerging virtual reality genre: *eXistenz* and *Thirteenth Floor* hoped to compete. Both films fell flat at the box office.

But *The Matrix* continued its rollicking success.

Ultimately, a quest for the roots of *The Matrix* could challenge seekers as

much as the quest of the movie itself. It is one more thing to bring viewers back to the movie again and again, finding things they did not see
before, understanding things they did not know before. The stories and
elements form part of the larger tapestry; knowing them, we can more
effectively examine the larger work itself.

One thing remains before we leave the question of influences and under-
pinnings: the consideration of myth and religion in *The Matrix*. Since the
Wachowski brothers have said that these sources lie at the heart of their
hopes for their films, let us give them some serious attention.

_4 //

_ E N L I G H T E N E D . . . F R O M
E A S T   T O   W E S T _

I am here, not because of the path that lies before me,
but because of the path that lies behind me.

MORPHEUS, in *Reloaded*

In *The Matrix*, the Wachowskis draw liberally on religious motifs, stories, and symbols in their pursuit of a working twenty-first-century myth.

"The Bible seeks to answer a lot of relevant questions for man," Larry told *Time*'s Richard Corliss. "Then there's the whole idea of a messiah. It's not just a Judeo-Christian myth; it also plays into the search for the reincarnation of the Buddha."[1]

Larry's statement implies how the film has placed itself into an entirely new genre, as a meta-story. Films like *Star Wars*, *The Apostle*, and *Life Is Beautiful* all draw from spiritual realities. But *The Matrix* draws from multiple dogmas and so entices and edifies viewers who embrace radically different faith perspectives.

NEO BUDDHA?

The movie's references to Buddhism begin with this idea of incarnation—or, rather, reincarnation, as one school of Buddhism expressly believes.

Followers of the current Dalai Lama, for example, believe him to be the reincarnation of earlier Dalai Lamas.

Neo is said to be the sixth in a string of possible "Ones"—reincarnated, if you will, from the first man who gained power over the matrix. The Oracle's words to Neo—"Maybe in your next life"—give further evidence of this idea of reincarnation. The only escape from the ongoing cycle, called in Buddhism *samsara*, comes by achieving enlightenment. Neo's entire experience is a quest for this enlightenment—to wake up, to see the world as it is, to recognize that it is not the spoon that bends, but himself.

When Neo achieves enlightenment at the end of the first film, he sees the matrix as a stream of green characters—the world as it is. When he achieves this mastery, natural laws no longer apply to him. The bullets the agents fire at him, for example, cannot harm him. Just as the fiery discus that the demon Mara fired at Gautama Buddha turned into harmless flowers as the Buddha sat contemplating under the Bodhi Tree, his place of enlightenment, so these bullets become beautiful, shiny objects that Neo can pluck from the air.

This power is prophesied earlier in the film when Morpheus talks with Neo about enlightenment. When Neo wonders aloud if he will be able to dodge bullets, Morpheus says, "I mean, when the time comes, you won't have to."

Upon achieving enlightenment, the enlightened one can take one of two possible avenues. He can leave behind this world—he can enter nirvana—or he can remain behind to try to enlighten others, and so bring peace to the world. This is Neo's choice at the end of *The Matrix*. And like the Buddha, who at the time of his enlightenment heard an entreaty by the god

Brahma to remain in this plane of existence on behalf of all created things, Neo chooses to return to the matrix, even though he has transcended it. Neo will now try to pass his path on to others, at least as much as he can. Maybe the other characters can't leap tall buildings in a single bound. But in *Reloaded*, he reminds the character called Kid that although he may have gotten the Kid out of the matrix, Neo didn't save him: "You saved yourself."

Clear differences exist between some of the core philosophies expressed in Buddhism and *The Matrix*. Violence, for example, is proscribed in most Buddhist beliefs, whereas in the film, violence is job one. But we need to remember that the Wachowski brothers are doing more than creating simple allegory. They do not intend Neo to represent the Buddha (as Keanu Reeves did in the film *Little Buddha*). And *The Matrix* is not simply a disguised retelling of his life. Still, recognizing correspondences between them enhances our understanding of the movie and the messages it contains.

The Matrix Goes to Sunday School

This is likewise true of the brothers' use of Judeo/Christian tradition. Some character names reveal a clear dependence.

Apoc, for example, plainly references the Apocalypse, the Christian view of end times. The *Nebuchadnezzar* is Morpheus' ship, instantly recalling the powerful Babylonian king who oppressed the people of Israel, conquered many nations, and ruled with an iron fist. Yet, his empire eventually fell while Israel found restoration. Malachi and Hamann, characters from *Reloaded*, evoke figures from the Hebrew Bible, while Niobe's ship, the *Logos*—the fastest in the fleet, according to the screenplay—is emblematic of the Word of God and the creation story.

As we will see in more detail through coming character studies, at various times Morpheus provides a figure of God the Father and also of John the Baptist; Neo of Jesus; Cypher of the betrayer, Judas Iscariot; and Trinity of the Holy Trinity of God the Father, God the Son, and God the Holy Spirit. The last human city, Zion, recalls the biblical holy city of God, a metaphor for God's reign on earth and in heaven.

An ancient offshoot of Christianity called Gnosticism supplies some of the clearest sources of myth in *The Matrix*. Though many Christians celebrate the biblical imagery in these films, it should be clear that the last thing Christians would desire is to be Gnostics. Like other mystery cults, Gnosticism required its initiates to pass through a time of "secret knowledge" in which they would gain enlightenment. The *gnostikoi*—the knowing ones—had, as Karen Armstrong declares, "turned from philosophy to mythology to explain their acute sense of separation from the divine world."[2] Like Plato, the Gnostics posited two worlds, the spiritual and the material. Gnostic writings, such as the *Gospel of Thomas*, often emphasize this distinction. In *Thomas*, Jesus says, "Wretched is the body that is dependent on a body and wretched is the soul that is dependent on them both." In this system, the image of pearls cast into the muck provides an apt metaphor for the condition of the spirit temporarily trapped in a fallen, material world. This is the center of Gnostic heresy, that the flesh is inherently evil—it eventually denies the core of Christianity, the incarnation.

Gnostic myths tell a story about the genesis of the universe very different from the one described in mainstream Judeo/Christian texts. Through some catastrophe, the spiritual power, *Sophia* (Wisdom), was dispelled from the divine world, *Pleroma*, like Satan from heaven. Her grief and distress created the world of matter. Other Gnostic legends account for the creation of the material world in similar ways, but all express the belief that this world—the one that we encounter through our senses, the one we believe to be real—is an inferior copy of the *Pleroma*, and that the highest God (who is unnamable and unknowable in most Gnostic myth) did not directly participate in its creation, "since he could have nothing to do with base matter."[3]

All is not lost, however; although humans populate this imperfect world, they can still find paths back to the Divine. "The Gnostic could find a divine spark in his own soul, could become aware of a divine element within himself which would help him find his way home."[4] The Gnostics believed that in the form of Jesus, another spiritual power, the *Logos*, descended to earth to show humankind the way to return to God. And what was that way? Remember that the Gnostics created a mystery cult. The secret knowledge of the Gnostics—the knowledge that would lead to enlightenment and redemption—consisted of the "secret history" (more precisely, a history kept secret from the uninitiated) of the origin and creation of the world, the origin of evil, the drama of the divine Redeemer come down to earth to save men, and the final victory of the transcendent God—a victory that would find expression in the conclusion of history and the annihilation of the cosmos.

The operating myth of *The Matrix* can be plainly seen here: a small group of initiates (represented primarily in the film by Morpheus and his crew) who have secret knowledge about the history and genesis of the world bring Thomas Anderson/Neo into the fold. They tell him this secret history, explain how evil entered the world (the pride of man as he creates Artificial Intelligence), and relate their belief in the One, a redeemer (Neo himself) who will save humankind and destroy the world of the matrix.

Among the best-known Gnostic images and symbols are amnesia (that is, forgetting or not knowing who you are), sleep, drunkenness, torpor, captivity, falling, and homesickness—most of which Neo experiences in his journey. The initial call to Neo to "wake up," and its continuing development in the story, remains central to the Gnostic experience. "Let him who hears wake from heavy sleep," says the *Apocalypse of John*, one of the Gnostic gospels. Gnosticism typically identifies sleep with ignorance and death. The wise Councillor Hamann in *Reloaded* puts it this way when Neo tells him he hasn't been able to sleep: it is a sign "that you are, in fact, still human."

In some Gnostic myths, the redeemer figure, like Neo, is actually *made* to forget who he is and what he knows. These stories tell how the transcendent being is "captured by demonic powers and, brutalized by immersion in matter, forgets his identity; God then sends a messenger who, by 'awakening' him, helps him recover consciousness of himself."[5] The image of Neo as we first see him in the generator pod, immersed in viscous liquid, and Neo's awakening (whether we think of it at the hands of Trinity, who hacks into his computer at the beginning of the film, or at the hands of Morpheus, who searches for him, finds him, and rescues him from the matrix and makes it possible for him to understand his true spiritual nature) clearly parallel this Gnostic story.

Neo's death at the hands of Agent Smith—his crucifixion, if you will—represents the final moment of awakening in the film, and the ultimate gnosis. Neo becomes the One. (The Gnostic *Gospel of Philip* describes this transformation as transcendent, as a being "no longer a Christian, but a Christ.") As a result of this final awakening, Neo becomes a creature of pure light that bursts apart Agent Smith from within.

The image of light appears often in Gnostic writings. In the *Apocalypse of Peter*, the resurrected Christ appears to Peter as an "intellectual spirit, filled with radiant light." In the *Gospel of Thomas*, Jesus says, "There is light within a man of light and it illuminates the whole world." Light represents the ultimate gnosis, repelling ignorance, awakening the sleeper, and banishing darkness. The screenplay for *Reloaded* emphasizes this idea when the *Nebuchadnezzar* arrives in Zion at last and "beams of celestial radiant light" guide the crew home.

In one major respect, *The Matrix* differs from its Gnostic influences. Unlike other early Christian sects, the Gnostics generally held that Jesus was not killed and reborn in his earthly body; perhaps he was reborn into a new spiritual body that appeared to Mary and the disciples. After all, why would a transcendent spirit return to a physical body?

The Matrix, however, clearly shows Neo's physical death—he flatlines aboard the ship and one of the Agents affirms, "He's gone"—and physical resurrection. The Neo that Trinity holds aboard the *Nebuchadnezzar* opens his eyes. Perhaps, however, the transformation within *The Matrix* that allows him to change from his "physical" matrix form into light corresponds to this Gnostic belief.

A RICH, MYTHOLOGICAL DENSITY

The *Matrix* films draw on stories and belief systems from across time, as the Wachowski brothers pull together familiar tales and obscure references. There are Buddhism and Greek myth, Gnostic teaching and mainstream Christianity. We'll be addressing Christian references and lessons throughout the rest of the book, but it's good to make a point here. We shouldn't try too hard to seek an exact correspondence between any of the religious references and images and story lines in *The Matrix*. This isn't the Gospel According to Larry and Andy, but, rather, a popular cultural artifact that explores religious and philosophical issues by creating a new pattern of myth.

The Matrix often has its cake and eats it, too, where mythology and religion are concerned. This density, in fact, is one of the things that makes the movie so compelling, so endlessly rich, and so open to multiple viewings and interpretations.

_5 //

_ P A R A D I S E   L O S T _

World's use is cold, world's love is vain, world's cruelty is bitter bane;
but is not the fruit of pain.

E L I Z A B E T H   B A R R E T T   B R O W N I N G

One might imagine that man, given the choice, would always choose pleasure over pain, heaven over hell, and joy over despair. Yet the story of mankind, whether in Genesis or the postmodern tapestry we call *The Matrix*, indicates something very different.

When Agent Smith tells Morpheus that the computer program called the matrix (the second matrix, as it turns out) represents the best reality his "primitive cerebrum" can comprehend — the "peak of your civilization" — he reveals *The Matrix* as a critique of modernity.

The created world serves as a satirical replica of the arrogance of modern man. The buildings tower to the sky, Agents use living organisms in surveillance of suspects, machines and software have advanced to a fantastic degree, and yet mankind lives in a state of chaos and depravity. Progress, as formerly imagined, turns out to be a fantasy.

The Heart of the City — the hotel where the film begins and ends its main action — is nothing but a dump, corroded from wear, a heart clogged and weakly beating.

The painful paradox seems palpable. Man has accomplished more than he ever dreamed possible. But this, the "height of his civilization" (as modernists would measure it), still comes up short. Mankind longed to be the Creator instead of the creation, and so it suffers a betrayal of its own making. The grandest accomplishment of mankind—artificial intelligence (A.I.)—also longs to rule, and so works to overthrow humanity, just as man sought to overthrow God, first in the Garden of Eden, and later through science and reason.

In this recurring story we find the eternal tension between Man and God, and thus Technology and Man. One Being in the garden stood superior to all others, and those others longed to be like him. So if human beings become the creators of intelligent life, then would that life, too, not long to become like its masters? And so the machines of this new world differ only in the slightest from the masters who came before. The Agents, their representatives, are as human as we—as cruel, as arrogant, as blind to suffering (in the films, for example, we repeatedly see Agents painfully "possess" humans in the matrix, only to toss them into deadly battles against Morpheus and his followers). The world the Machines have created—both within the matrix and without, in the "desert of the real"—is simply our world, with our human faults writ large.

CREATED FOR PARADISE

This is not the world for which we were intended. God did not create humanity for war, hostility, pain, labor, and depression. In the story of the Garden of Eden, beauty surrounds mankind. Food abounds, labor remains nameless, and pleasure shows up as the only item on the daily agenda. Man and woman walk with their Creator in the evening shadows, known by him and loved by him. Everything is right with the world.

And yet humankind was not happy with what it had. In the Genesis account—and in many others from many cultures—humans reject a perfect world by grasping for more, for something beyond paradise. How could people possibly reject peace, gratification, and leisure, in favor of war, hostility, and pain?

"As-s-s-s-piration," whispers the snake.

It is the predicament of humanity. We want what we do not have, and in the process of gaining it, we measure our accomplishment.

In the story of the Tower of Babel recorded in the book of Genesis, humans express the conceit that building a tall tower—a building to the sky—will make them equal to God. Perhaps this desire lies behind much of our striving, but it certainly seems to have skewed our priorities. We measure ourselves by our surface accomplishments, by what we build (or what we make, in more contemporary terms)—but how does this measure what we make *of* ourselves? God himself weighed in on the Babel-builders: "No telling what they'll come up with next—they'll stop at nothing,"[1] he said, and fearing the disastrous effects such a skewed belief would have on his deluded creatures, he made it impossible for them to communicate with each other, thus scorching their project.

On a less divine note, Douglas Adams wrote in *The Hitchhiker's Guide to the Galaxy*, "Man had always assumed that he was more intelligent than dolphins because he had achieved so much . . . the wheel, New York, wars, and so on, whilst all the dolphins had ever done was muck about in the water having a good time. But conversely the dolphins believed themselves to be more intelligent than man for precisely the same reasons."[2] If we arrive at the seventh heaven, we will quickly tire of it unless someone organizes a cloud-sculpting contest.

Even as we humans enjoyed the naked bliss of the garden, we could not resist the opportunity to screw the whole thing up. Adam and Eve did not despise paradise; that was never the problem. They simply wanted *more*.

And so it is with the matrix. As he prepares to destroy Morpheus' mind, Agent Smith reminds his captive of humanity's limitations by giving him a history lesson unwritten in any human book or hard drive: "The first matrix was designed to be a perfect human world where none suffered, where everyone would be happy. It was a disaster. No one would accept the program."

The comment gives us pause for a number of reasons. First, of course, we bump into the problem of ultimate goodness, or perfection. As we try to project our own human ideas to create possible heavens, we cannot help but fail miserably; our human words, concepts, and experiences fall woefully short of portraying such transcendence. It seems just about as unlikely that devout Christians will be walking streets of gold and playing banjos encrusted with precious stones as devout Muslims will enter a lush garden filled with date palms and willing maidens—but these visions are the best we can do when we try to imagine what we think of as the Highest Good, an existence lived in direct, unmediated communion with God. We cannot begin to fathom the concept of heaven. "There I was in paradise," Paul wrote, "and heard things so astounding that they are beyond a man's power to describe or put in words."[3]

And perhaps, in our human state—as when we enjoyed direct communion with God—we won't be able to accept it.

Will we enjoy heaven or continue in our patterns to seek out a little bit of hell so that we know we're still alive? Samuel Coleridge once said,

"Real pain can alone cure us of imaginary ills. We feel a thousand miseries till we are lucky enough to feel misery." In his novel, *The Count of Monte Cristo*, French writer Alexandre Dumas wrote that suffering makes us happy: "There is neither happiness nor unhappiness in this world. There is only the comparison of one state with another. Only a man who has felt the ultimate despair is capable of feeling ultimate bliss. It is necessary to have wished for death . . . in order to know how good it is to live."

Such is the state of things in this world. We seem unable to tolerate too much of either extreme without wishing for escape.

DEFINE YOUR EXISTENCE THROUGH PAIN

Can't live with it, can't live without it. Sometimes it seems that humanity has *chosen* pain. In fact, we choose it every day.

Whenever we lack the wisdom to make sound choices, or we give in to selfish desires, we choose pain. In our attachment to temporal things, we choose pain. Even in our attachment to those we love—perhaps among our most divine qualities—we choose pain. And even when we don't choose pain, it seems to come upon us through the simple circumstances of life. Things change.

The story of Job in the Hebrew Bible, one of the most ancient and disturbing texts in that ancient collection, describes the tragedies visited on Job, a faithful servant of God. He was spared nothing because of his faith—none of us are, ultimately. Life in this world always involves loss.

As Job's friends ruminated on what he had done or left undone, Job grew increasingly testy. At last, when Job dared to wonder aloud why

God would permit him to suffer so intensely, God told him that, frankly, it is none of his business. It's just the way things are. "Where were you when I laid the foundations of the universe?" he asked Job. A definite conversation killer.

Things are the way they are. Life is pain, as the hero of another movie, *The Princess Bride*, tells us. Or in the words of Francis Thompson, "Nothing begins, and nothing ends, that is not paid with moan; for we are born in other's pain, and perish in our own."

When, in the beginning, humankind chose complication and pain over simple paradise, God decreed, "I'll multiply your pains in childbirth; you'll give birth to your babies in pain."[4] So we begin our lives through pain and we end them in pain, and perhaps, as Thomas Jefferson said, "The art of life is the art of avoiding pain."

We make choices every day that will inevitably return to us with consequences to test our strength and character. If the pain feels overwhelming, we may go see a therapist, talk through the pain, weep, find solace, confess. But mostly, it seems, we seek all sorts of modern refuges: in food, Prozac, booze, chocolate, caffeine, adventure, mindless sex, cocaine, or nicotine. Anything to numb us, to take the edge off, if only for a moment.

PEAK OF YOUR CIVILIZATION

Again, Agent Smith: "So the perfect world was a dream that your primitive cerebrum kept trying to wake up from. Which is why the matrix was redesigned to this, the peak of your civilization."

Look around you now, as you read this. Chances are that unless you've climbed high into the mountains of the Sierra Madre or have camped along a primitive beach, you are at this moment surrounded by the trappings of modern society. And yet, with everything we have built—everything that helps us gauge our success, our intelligence, our resourcefulness—what have we accomplished?

True, at no other time could we travel so quickly from one place to the other, transmit information from one person to another, blast payload from our planet into the void of space. But what have we done with all this science and technology? We travel to exotic places where we refuse to open ourselves to their true essence, for fear of what we might learn. The fact that a person can travel from anywhere to anywhere else has become as much a matter of fear as of pride. With the magic powers of the Internet, we could be transmitting recipes for peace—or at least for really good chocolate chip cookies—but instead we waste bandwidth transmitting pornography and spewing racial hatred and invective. And the technology to blast into space? It can just as easily launch nuclear missiles and spy satellites.

In the film *Contact*, based on the work of the late astronomer Carl Sagan, the first bit of information an alien race learns of earthmen comes in a television transmission featuring Adolf Hitler. As King Solomon said, "There is nothing new under the sun."

We know the news before it becomes news. We hear the murmurs of hungry stomachs in India and see the ravages of AIDS in sub-Saharan Africa. We see the deaths of untold men and women in war-torn Chechnya and Bosnia. But knowing the news has become more a curse than a blessing, for our technology simply amplifies and multiplies our pain.

With all our power, with all our technology, have we progressed a centimeter from those Stone Age savages whom God saw piling rocks to heaven? We have better tools; we have more power at our hands. This is the peak of our civilization.

But look what a mess we've made of things.

HUMANITY AS VIRUS

When Morpheus sits waiting in the tower for his death, Agent Smith works to peel back the layers of his resistance by mocking his humanity. "There is another organism on this planet," he says, "that follows the same pattern [as humanity]: a virus. Human beings are a disease, a cancer of this planet. You are a plague, and we are the cure."

While we dislike his words, we also recognize some truth here. Who would deny that we could be a better people? We *could* find equilibrium with the planet and with one another. But since our exile from the garden, humankind has wanted more, has spread across the surface of the planet expanding and exploiting, until it seems clear that we are likely to kill our planet unless we change our ways . . . or something stops us. The catastrophic powers of destruction that warring factions now have in hand could do incalculable damage to the ecosystem, to all the living systems that share the globe with us. Nuclear winter from a series of nuclear explosions could blot out the sun and plunge the earth into untold years of cold, as in *The Matrix*. Unchecked industrialization could raise the level of greenhouse gases until the icecaps melt, coastlines disappear under water, and Northern cities swelter. Or it could create a level of toxicity in our air and water that dooms other organisms . . . and eventually, us.

Like a virus, we seem to have little concern for our host, the earth. Single-celled viruses have no intelligence and no concept of a future. But we do. So why do we act this way?

Well, like the hungry viruses to which Agent Smith compares us, our internal workings—our powerful emotions of greed and hatred—spur us on. If a virus gained sentience for a moment, aware enough to realize that it was destroying its host and itself with it, what would it say?

More to the point—what should *we* say?

As we've seen, the world of *The Matrix* is our world, even down to this first rejection of a "perfect matrix" in favor of a world as screwed up as the one we have. And only some kind of intervention, some divine reaching across the waves, can bring us back into harmony—can make us feel harmony—with a perfect good. John Milton took this as his subject in *Paradise Lost*:

> Of Man's First Disobedience, and the Fruit
> Of that Forbidden Tree, whose mortal taste
> Bought Death into the World, and all our woe
> With loss of Eden, Till one greater Man
> Restore us, and regain the blissful Seat . . .

In chapter 7, we'll take another look at that disastrous separation—and what's necessary to restore us to the blissful Seat.

_6//

_ N E O :   M Y   O W N   P E R S O N A L   J E S U S _

"The hour is come, that the Son of man should be glorified."

JOHN 12:23

Most people don't expect the Messiah to look, act, or talk like Keanu Reeves. We have a hard time imagining that Jesus ever said, "Whoa!"

But perhaps that's part of the point in casting Reeves in the role of Neo. Messiahs may come from where you least expect them, and all of us have the capacity to grow and advance as spiritual beings.

SOMEONE SPECIAL

The conversation between Cypher and Trinity that begins the action in *The Matrix* gives us our first hint that someone special is out there.

"Morpheus believes he is the One," Trinity tells the cynical Cypher— and we're inclined to grant her some leeway after we see the way she can take out an armed police squad and fly across streetscapes. But still, it comes as something of a shock to look at the sleeping Thomas Anderson/Neo and connect her reverence with such an obviously imperfect vessel.

Yet it seems clear that the Wachowski brothers mean for us to connect Neo with Jesus Christ; he forms part of the Trinity of Morpheus/God the Father and Trinity/the Holy Spirit. Still, it shouldn't surprise us that lots of people—and not just audience members—react with some skepticism to the idea. We learn Neo is one of a string of possible messiahs, none of whom have yet survived the stringent, fake-messiah-weeding-out program.

Things were no different in Jesus' time.

A LOOK AT PARALLELS

Surrounding the time of Christ, a number of candidates for the Jewish Messiah, whether rabbis or prophets or itinerant preachers of peace and justice, arrived on the scene.

Some thought John the Baptist might be the Messiah; others pitched their tents behind the Essene leader known as the Teacher of Righteousness (even though neither man claimed to be anything more than a messenger paving the way). Certainly the Jews needed a messiah, and more than a few no doubt thought, *Hey, today would not be too early*. But always, without exception, this or that messiah proved to be merely a man. So it's no wonder that the Jews—like the crew of Morpheus' ship—had grown fed up with the waiting. They slid into doubt and began to lose hope and faith.

Neo's given name, Thomas A. Anderson, resonates with importance. As many observers have pointed out, we remember Thomas as the doubting disciple, the one who demanded physical proof that Jesus was indeed the Christ. The *Gospel of Thomas* remains one of the most important and best known in the Gnostic collection, and we've seen how the *Matrix* movies often use Gnostic images and symbols. And the last name, Anderson, translates into "Son of Man," the term Jesus customarily used for himself during his ministry.

Several times the film uses Neo's full name: Thomas A. Anderson. It's here that we can understand one of the clear points of the film and its approach to Neo as Messiah. Thomas, a Son of Man—we might read this to say, "My character as a doubter is part of my becoming, and I am one of many possible messiahs."

The Wachowskis do not want us to believe that Neo is Jesus—clearly he isn't—but rather, they want us to take away some spiritual lessons by thinking of him in a Jesus-style role. One of those lessons seems to be this: Jesus perfectly fused God and man, incarnated the divine, and thus represented the highest spiritual advancement imaginable for humans. He also set an example for us and gave us a sample of what we might achieve. As much as Jesus was God, he also was fully man, prone at least potentially to the same annoying habits of sloth and disbelief that plague us—yet possessing the keys to redemption.

The first linking of Neo to Jesus comes after Neo's initial wake-up call, when his hacker friend greets him: "Hallelujah! You're my savior, man, my own personal Jesus Christ." This sets a pattern of reference that extends throughout the film—often, interestingly enough, through cursing to or about Neo. For example, during Neo's training bout with Morpheus, Mouse says, "Jesus Christ, he's fast." And after he asks Neo if he knows why they brought him out, Cypher says to him, "Jesus, what a mind job." No other character has this pattern of cursing attached to him (or her) and no one utters what seems like a curse using the name "Jesus" except in connection with Neo. It seems to be a conscious choice on the directors' part. In fact, in the 1996 draft of the screenplay, the policeman who reacts with amazement to the Agent's leap to another building—"That's impossible"—originally prefaced his statement with "Jesus Christ," a bit of dialogue dropped from the shooting script and the film.

Neo also has a tempter—Cypher, offering illicit hootch and unwise advice—as Jesus had Satan. Likewise, Neo has a betrayer in his inner circle—Cypher again—as Jesus had Judas. And in each case of betrayal, the seeming victory for the forces of authority and conventionality actually serves as part of a larger plan. The betrayal actually puts divine grace into action.

Neo's ministry can be traced, like that of Jesus, through the progress of miracles. His first apparent miracle—dodging bullets on the rooftop—might be compared to Jesus turning water into wine. Trinity doesn't fall on her face and worship Neo; she simply asks, "How did you do that?" We can almost imagine Jesus' friends tugging their beards and saying something similar. This first miracle for each man might tempt some observers to think, *parlor trick.*

But then, when Neo rescues Morpheus, the miraculous big guns come into play, something like Jesus bringing Lazarus back to life. "Come forth, Lazarus," even sounds something like Neo's urging Morpheus out of his jailhouse room to life. Neither can be explained in any sort of rational way. After Neo's exploits in the rescue of Morpheus, the others recognize him as the One; those who watched Jesus at the tomb of Lazarus cast away any thoughts of him as a pretender.

The last great miracle for both, of course, is resurrection. Both die, remain dead for a period of time, and return to life to continue their ministries. In each case, the figure of the Holy Spirit breathes life back into them (the actual breath of God in the case of Jesus, the figurative breath of God in the form of Trinity for Neo) and they arise reborn, transformed, transfigured. No longer subject to the mundane laws of human existence, they yet remain a little longer in order to pass on their teachings.

THE PROBLEM OF VIOLENCE

We run into one major problem with this Neo/Jesus comparison and we have to face it (later we will dissect it in more detail). How can we identify the Glock-wielding Neo as the cross-bearing Prince of Peace?

Allow us to suggest several lines of explanation.

First, remember that this is a Hollywood action movie; no one will mistake it for Martin Scorsese's *Kundun*. Genre movies like the *Matrix* trilogy rely on the convention of action to attract an audience, and the Wachowski brothers conceived of the movies in this way—as thoughtful films that attract and entertain an audience in part through wild flights of gunplay.

But we also can remember that the Prince of Peace reacted with controlled violence when he saw injustice or personal violation. Although we don't usually tend to remember him in this way, picture in your mind an angry Jesus overturning the tables of moneylenders and running them out of the temple with a whip in his hands. In the face of some things, Jesus didn't turn the other cheek; he got busy.

We might also remember a statement of Jesus that we find in the New Testament: "Do not suppose that I have come to bring peace to the earth. I did not come to bring peace, but a sword."[1] The *Gospel of Thomas* remembered his words like this: "People think it is for peace I have come into the world, but they do not know it is dissension I have come to cast

on the earth: fire, sword, war." Whether we think of this statement literally or figuratively, the message of Jesus—and the message of the *Matrix*
films—is nothing but radical. It opposes traditional power in support of
the downtrodden. And it brings conflict into the open.

No man can serve two masters. Everyone has to choose sides, and Jesus
left no room for compromise. Such an unyielding approach—"Our way
or the highway," as Switch puts it—creates conflict. And in the films, violence symbolizes that conflict.

As much as we admire Dr. Martin Luther King, Jr. and Desmond Tutu,
nonviolent civil disobedience simply won't work on the machines of the
matrix. The Agents will simply shut you down and the system will feed
you to the next guy.

FINAL LESSONS

Whether we think of the Messiah/the One as someone who achieves
perfection or as someone who simply recognizes his own divinity (we
know theological distinctions must be drawn here; just stick with us), all
of us can find hope.

Maybe we can't be Jesus. Maybe we can't be Neo. We don't expect to fly
through the streets at two thousand miles an hour, as Neo does in
Reloaded. But like Neo, we can move from doubt and fear to faith and the
possibility of transcendence.

And really, if Keanu Reeves can aspire to spiritual greatness, why can't
anyone?

_7 //

_ L E A P   O F   F A I T H

It takes a leap of faith to get things started.

BRUCE SPRINGSTEEN

When the first *Matrix* film begins, we feel immediately drawn into the downward swoosh of the camera. We descend into the digits of a phone number appearing on the trace program, and then the camera drops down once more to the sign of a hotel from which Trinity is calling. Such visual motifs of falling set a pattern for the entire movie.

The Matrix is a film about overcoming the fear of falling and taking a leap of faith, ascending instead of dropping. From the computer commanding Neo to wake up, to his soaring off the ground and into the camera in the last frames of the film, we follow—and learn about—the ascent of a spirit through belief and the conquering of disbelief.

HEIGHTS = DANGER AND LOSS OF CONTROL

The film begins with a frenetic chase scene across the rooftops (reversed at the end of the film, with Neo running back to the hotel instead of away, as Trinity does). As in Alfred Hitchcock's films, especially *Vertigo*, heights are meant to convey danger and loss of control. (This continues to be true in

Reloaded, which begins with Neo's dream of Trinity falling to her death.)

Even after Trinity defeats the police who come to arrest her and we see the first discomfiting use of "bullet time," it still might be possible for us to imagine we are watching an action movie set in an ordinary world. In *Vertigo*—or in *Lethal Weapon IV*, for that matter—police pursue criminals, make leaps, pull themselves up after slips and misjumps.

But then, as Trinity and the Agent pull away from the puffing policemen across the rooftops, something happens: Trinity leaps across an impossible gap between buildings, falling, rolling. The pursuing Agent leaps high into the air and comes down with a solid thud—and one of the policemen declares what we are feeling: "That's impossible."

For humans like us—and like them—it is. Only supernatural Agents and enlightened humans can make such a leap with any chance of success. Without training—without believing that it is not impossible—it is and always will be.

You Have to Believe

Morpheus does not train Neo in order to teach him kung fu, as we will see in a later chapter (however important martial arts knowledge becomes in the film). He offers, rather, spiritual training, trying to replace years of dogma and blinders with a new, if frightening, way of understanding the world. "I am trying to make you see," Morpheus tells Neo. He tries to make Neo push past "fear, doubt, and disbelief."

As Neo begins to learn his lessons, he takes his first major leap. In the dojo simulation, he runs up the beam, somersaults in beautiful, wire-supported slow motion—and promptly gets kicked into another pillar by Morpheus. However amazing the feat seems to us filmgoers, it illustrates how a little understanding can be a dangerous thing. A mustard seed of faith makes the unattainable a reality—and a dangerous risk.

When Neo demonstrates to Morpheus that he can hit him—thus showing that theoretically, at least, he can master the knowledge that Morpheus possesses—Tank loads the jump program, a test familiar to all of the *Nebuchadnezzar's* crew. (Whether they themselves have made the jump or merely have witnessed the jumps of others remains unclear. Yet it stretches our credibility to imagine that some of the crew—Cypher in particular—might have succeeded.)

"Free your mind," Morpheus instructs Neo—and then the teacher disappears, soaring across the city to a distant building. "No one makes it the first time," the crew tells us, and yet they dare to hope that Neo can be the first, that he has reached a point of mastery that will let him follow Morpheus. Neo himself half-believes he can do it, giving himself a pep talk. But half-belief is not enough—halfway across, Neo does a Wile E. Coyote plunge into the concrete canyons below (another cartoon nod from the Wachowski brothers). Dogma—like the law of gravity, for example—still holds too much sway over Neo and his thoughts.

After the jump program, Morpheus takes Neo to the Oracle, where his lack of faith once again becomes obvious (especially when contrasted against Morpheus' faith in him and the possibilities now open to him). Neo does not allow the Oracle even to proclaim the truth. He fills it in for her: "But I'm not the One." And the Oracle's follow-up—that Neo knew she would say that very thing—could be as much about Neo's lack of faith as about any judgment she planned to render. To be the One, one has to believe he is the One.

In the subsequent firefight, Morpheus sacrifices himself to help Neo escape. Yet Neo does not fight back—in fact, he gets unceremoniously dragged down the wet wall and falls into the basement with as little grace as he displayed in the jump program. Again using the movie's visual metaphors of rising and falling, Neo reinforces the Oracle's (and his) prediction: he is not the One.

VICTORY THROUGH FAITH

The film proclaims that the fight is not won with might or skill. Victory comes through faith. And so in this key respect the film echoes the Bible's magnificent stories of God bringing triumph in battle to his believing people.

This only makes sense, for if the narrator of the biblical story (God) has ultimate power, then right should always win out, at least in the end. As the Israelites prepared to enter the Promised Land under the leadership of Joshua, for example, the old general pondered the wonder of God's power in battle: "Think of it—one of you, single-handedly, putting a thousand on the run! Because GOD is GOD, your God. Because he fights for you, just as he promised you."[1] Those words take form as Neo slays hundreds of Agent Smiths in *Reloaded*.

Preparation for battle is all about leaving behind doubt and disbelief. It must be excised from your mind (or from your crew—maybe Neo's leap of faith finally comes because the doubter, Cypher, gets dispelled from their midst). In advancing this theory, consider another biblical example. God told Gideon to scale back his troops as they prepared to face a formidable army: "Make a public announcement: 'Anyone afraid, anyone who has any qualms at all, may leave Mount Gilead now and go home.'"

In response, twenty-two companies headed for home while only ten companies remained.[2] More than two thirds of the soldiers deserted their peers—and this unlikely turn of events is precisely the thing that prepared Gideon's army for success. Eventually God had Gideon pare down his fighting force to just three hundred men, armed with nothing more than trumpets, jars, torches—and faith. Yet, so equipped, they destroyed a massive army.

Imagine what might have happened had they marched into battle with a large, but fearful army. Would doubt have doomed their fight?

RISING AFTER A FALL

A lack of faith seemed to doom Neo as well. Yet when it seems that all hope is lost, our hero faces his uncertainty. Neo falls as low as he can go, and then he begins to rise.

We also lose faith or ignore it until we find ourselves confronted with something beyond our ability to cope. God can disappear off our radar for weeks, months. But when we need help, suddenly we discover—or rediscover—faith. It isn't one of the prettiest aspects of human nature, but there it is.

And so it is with Neo, although the movie perhaps makes his faith more heroic than ours. When he decides he wants to rescue Morpheus, he has no demonstrable reason to think he can succeed. The Oracle has told him he isn't the One; Tank tells him he is loco. He has not fired a gun, thrown a punch outside a simulation, or confronted an Agent face-to-face. But his despair allows him to receive a divine epiphany. "It looks like suicide," he says back onboard the ship. "But it's not."

So Jesus might have remarked as he confronted the Crucifixion. Here is divine perspective, or at least the beginning of it.

Back to *The Matrix*. "What do you need, besides a miracle?" Tank asks. Well, of course, a miracle would be nice. Most of us would take a miracle. But it's not enough, and here's why: it doesn't require us to *do* anything. It doesn't require our participation in salvation. There's a prayer in the Reformed Jewish tradition that goes like this: "We should pray as if everything depends on God, and live as if everything depends on us."

Neo must put his faith into practice—and when spiritual warfare takes place in the *Matrix* films, it takes only one form. So what does Neo ask for?

"Guns," he says. And lots of them.

Neo's growing faith—"He is beginning to believe," Morpheus will later say—is reflected in the walls of guns, a hyperbolic and completely unbelievable armory of the spirit. Jesus said that if you had faith the size of a mustard seed you could move mountains—and this scene provides something of a visual equivalent. Faith has the power to rescue. One with an armory of a thousand angels can get ready for action—if only he believes.

FAITH LEAPS

Neo does indeed believe. During the rescue sequence that makes up the last third of *The Matrix*, we see a series of leaps, each of them important and symbolic.

To save Morpheus, Neo leaps from the helicopter. His willingness to dangle over the city—and then rescue Trinity from her falling fate—symbolizes Neo's newfound faith. It is immature but unmistakable and represents the first time someone clearly says that Neo is the One.

In the subway, Neo leaps toward Agent Smith at the beginning of their fight and then leaps out of the way of the oncoming train to defeat Smith—however momentarily. These leaps of faith show Neo taking on power he previously believed lay beyond him. Cypher has told Neo to run if he ever encounters an Agent, and Neo knows that nobody—not even Morpheus—has ever defeated an Agent.

The second leap represents another acceptance, for it follows Neo's assumption of his name—an important symbolic step. He is no longer Thomas A. Anderson. "My name," he says, "is Neo," and almost with these words, he jumps high enough to bang Agent Smith loose against the ceiling and then vaults impossibly out of the way of the approaching train—"the sound of inevitability," as Smith had called it. "The sound of your death."

Neo no longer accepts that he has to die. And when Smith beats him to Room 303 in the hotel, Neo raises his hand to his chest after Smith shoots him, similar to the way he once raised his hand to the back of his head to see if he had an input jack there. His faith has become so complete that he is unwilling to believe the believable—that if he is shot, bullets will pierce his flesh.

At the end of the film, one final leap occurs. A resurrected Neo leaps down the hallway and into Agent Smith, proving his power to destroy the matrix and to transcend its rules. Now it is Agent Smith who responds with disbelief, his understandings about the world of the matrix destroyed.

When Neo speaks into the telephone at the end of the first film, we hear the first words of this person of faith. Conversion is a reality. It is a beginning, he says. He does not know where things will go from here. But we do know one thing—as Neo soars toward and past us, it's clear that the only place for a leaping person to go is up.

Some years ago Greg met author and civil rights activist Maya Angelou at Baylor University, and in the course of their conversation, she said something that surprised him. "I am not a Christian," she told him. "I am trying to be a Christian."

At the time, he didn't understand. It seemed a rejection of what he thought Christianity was. But at last, he got it. Accepting is a powerful moment; it is, in fact, for many, the pivotal moment. In Christianity, the moment of decision has eternal significance. But as the films highlight, living as a person of faith is an ongoing work. And there is the trial, the joy, and the ultimate victory.

_ 8 //

_ REINVENTING MYTH FOR NEW GENERATIONS _

*We need myths that will identify the individual
not with his local group but with the planet.*

JOSEPH CAMPBELL, *The Power of Myth*

The Matrix is more than a hodgepodge of popular culture influences and striking genre revisions. The movie draws on myth, legend, and religion to reveal the Wachowski brothers' deepest desires for the *Matrix* films: to make us think about who we are, where we come from, and what we are supposed to be.

To create a new myth.

It is possible to experience these films simply for what they offer on the surface: action, romance, and a plethora of fashion tips. Some *Matrix* fans may think Plato is a moldable toy for kids that comes in a little yellow can. Do we have to disrupt their world and delve into the mind-bending philosophies that undergird this postmodern epic? No, but it is a rare occasion when a Hollywood blockbuster opens the door for learning found previously only in a master's-level philosophy course. If you love *The Matrix*, then journeying deep into these ideas will not only fill your mind with facts, you will likely learn the elements necessary to a truly great story and the reasons you feel drawn to this masterpiece.

THE POWER OF STORY

As Larry Wachowski pointed out in his *Time* magazine interview with Richard Corliss, the brothers felt drawn to myths and theology because they are "ways human beings try to answer bigger questions, as well as the Big Question."[1] Clearly the brothers think of myth in the same ways that late religion professor Joseph Campbell did—as a collection of codes, mores, experiences, and insights that we hold in common as human beings.

Some describe the use of symbol and mythology in these films as pure genius, pointing to a tapestry filled with power and meaning never before condensed to the space of a two-hour movie. But it is also possible that the brothers have used the sacred as a tool for unholy means, and in doing so, have dishonored the sacred signs of many cultural and religious traditions.

In *Reloaded* we get a brief glimpse of the hollowing out of what was once sacred. The camera pans to a back alley in Chinatown where street merchants have commodified what used to be holy. The shooting script describes the scene "where merchants are peddling the ultimate simulacra; spiritual and historic symbols, once powerful images now reduced to plastic, laminated bric-a-brac." In an article for *The Stranger*, Rick Levin observes this very same phenomenon at a large Christian rock festival. Read how he describes the abundance of holy merchandise:

> The Gorge was literally transformed for the weekend into an impromptu strip mall for Christ, with eager shoppers partaking in a variety of blatant consumer activities, each one underwritten by God and bearing the consistent trademark of a muscular and belligerent Jesus Christ. The catch phrase of Creation '99 was "Whoever takes the Son, takes it all." This aphorism states perfectly the overarching theme of the festival. Forget the stuff about

camels squeezing through the eyes of needles and the difficulties
of rich people getting past the pearly gates; access to heaven is on
a strictly cash-and-carry basis these days. Beneath the broad tents
set up throughout the grounds there were Christian entrepre-
neurs hawking all manner of Jesus gew-gaws: T-shirts, bumper
stickers, glow-in-the-dark crucifixes, Bibles, interpretations of the
Bible, compact discs, key chains, and jewelry.

The incredible adaptability of Christianity to modern mar-
keting techniques was fully evidenced in the logo-mongering
and sloganeering that marked these products. The phrases and
sayings emblazoned on the clothing at such places as the
"Know God" tent ("Christian Apparel with an Attitude")
promulgated that brand of neo-Christianity which touts Jesus
as a buff, ass-kicking man of combat, waging an eternal battle
against Satan. This iconic appeal to such gross capitalist sensibil-
ities is one of the most tragic aspects of modern Christianity's
loss of substance. Christ, as a spiritual product, has undergone a
stunning military-industrial make-over, emptied of content and
shrink-wrapped for the television generation. That this transformation has been enacted by the very same people who so
righteously wave the banner of "family values" is beyond ironic.
It's sick. It's everything Mark Twain and Friedrich Nietzsche
ever feared about the Christian church—greed and hypocrisy
masquerading as righteousness.[2]

If the story of God is used for selfish gain, over time its power gets diluted.
After decades of self-interested televangelists, it is no wonder that emerging generations yawn in the face of historic practices of faith and the
authority of the church.

That is, until *The Matrix*. Neo is a savior worth considering, and his recontextualization of the gospel as a story of freeing the captives has won many new believers.

REWORKING THE MYTHS

Unfortunately, as Campbell pointed out, many of the old myths are disappearing. Moreover, myths have to be constantly updated to speak afresh to new generations.

In a conversation with director George Lucas, Bill Moyers declared, "Joseph Campbell once said that all the great myths, the ancient great stories have to be regenerated in every generation. He said that's what you are doing with *Star Wars*." Lucas replied affirmatively: "I consciously set about to re-create myths and the classic mythological motifs. I wanted to use those motifs to deal with issues that exist today. The more research I did, the more I realized that the issues are the same ones that existed three thousand years ago."[3]

The Wachowskis also consciously set out to represent and rework these myths through the medium of the movies, which Richard Schickel refers to as a "living mythology." The story of Neo seeking to rescue a world in bondage represents the Wachowskis' attempt to bring healing to a confused world by reinjecting a common narrative. The biblical narrative's fall from prominence has left a vacuum in the culture—a space not easily filled. Moyers concurs: "The central ethic of our culture has been the Bible. . . . But the Bible no longer occupies that central place in our culture today. Young people in particular are turning to movies for their inspiration, not to organized religion."[4]

So the fact that the Wachowskis approach their storytelling with serious-ness—with a sense of what shared story can do for human beings and the goal of increasing their audiences' accessibility to the power of myth—makes the *Matrix* films especially important. Myth of any kind enlarges our humanity, shows us possible paths to follow, and gives us models for faith and hope.

THE MATRIX AND THE GREEKS

The Wachowskis clearly use classical mythology to shape their story. "We have Orpheus and Morpheus in the film," Larry says, and one can almost hear a touch of pride in his voice.[5]

Morpheus is the Greek god of dreams; his counterpart in *The Matrix* tells Neo that he's been living in a dream world and wakes him into the world of the real, for better or worse. In *The Metamorphoses*, by the Latin poet Ovid, we find another Morpheus (unrelated to the Greek god), whose name means, "he who forms, or molds," one more clear correspondence with the character in the *Matrix* films who, through tutelage and self-sacrifice, helps shape Neo's becoming.

The Greek hero and legendary singer Orpheus, who descends into the underworld to rescue his beloved, clearly parallels our Morpheus, who enters the world of the matrix to free Neo. Orpheus is later murdered by a group of orgiastic cult priestesses of the Greek god Dionysus—but despite his body being torn to pieces, his head continues to sing. Perhaps the Wachowski brothers recall this section of the Greek myth in the extreme close-ups of Morpheus' head during his captivity in the tower. Joseph Campbell notes that the Orpheus figure is often considered a pagan precursor to the later sacrificial Christ; and without Morpheus' sacrifice (the Oracle predicts that Morpheus will give his life to save Neo's), the human race cannot find redemption from the matrix.

Orpheus is also considered the "founder" of the Greek mystery cult of Orphism, which has many correspondences to the beliefs expressed in *The Matrix*. Mystery cults, as Campbell observed, shifted emphasis from "the purely phenomenal aspect of one's life to the spiritual, the deep, the energetic, the eternal aspect."[6] The Orphics believed that the soul was "shut up in the body (*soma*) as in a tomb (*sema*). Hence incarnate existence is more like a death,"[7] and the end of the body represents the beginning of life and the freeing of the soul.

As Neo is rescued from the matrix and "dies" to the world, freedom becomes possible for him—a salvation that comes through his initiation into revelations about the true nature of the universe and of the soul.

The Orphics also practiced vegetarianism in a rejection of the blood sacrifices that had gone before (perhaps symbolized in the film by the machines' characterization of humans as "batteries"). Cypher's choice of a thick, juicy steak as his meal with Agent Smith represents a clear break with the crew—and the mystery practice—and so emphasizes his betrayal.

Other significant Orphic beliefs concern reincarnation, a belief in a creator God, asceticism, and the divinity of man. All these ideas had great influence on the Western world (through Plato, and later, in the Christian era, the Neo-Platonists) and continue to influence us today (as we can see through the expression of these ideas in *The Matrix*). Although later faiths such as Christianity attacked the mystery cults—perhaps symbolized in the film by Agent Smith's characterization of Morpheus as the most dangerous man alive—their ideas did not disappear and were often syncretized or assimilated into later beliefs. As Mircea Eliade notes, "Orpheus is one of the very few Greek mythical figures that Europe, whether Christian, rationalistic, romantic, or modern, has not been willing to forget."[8]

In the character of the Oracle, the Wachowski brothers seem to be referring to the supernatural seers to whom the Greeks sometimes turned for answers—and whose answers often sounded as puzzling as the questions presented to them. These riddling answers—or amphibologies, as they were called—often became clear only after the events they prophesied had taken place. The Oracle's statement to Neo that he seems to be "waiting for something . . . maybe your next life" becomes clear only when Neo dies and is reborn at the end of the film. Only then does he completely become the One.

The most famous of the Greek oracles was undoubtedly the oracle at Delphi, consecrated to Apollo, god of the sun. It was this Delphic oracle that gave Oedipus the puzzling prophecy he understood only after its fulfillment—that he would kill his father and marry his mother. Inscribed at the site of the Delphic oracle (as on the platter over the Oracle's kitchen door) is the Latin for "know thyself." The Delphic oracle was said to inhale smoke, like the cigarette-smoking Oracle in the film, and to sit on a stool near a chasm from which an inspiring vapor rose. The Oracle of *The Matrix* sits on a stool next to the oven door waiting on her cookies ("Smell good, don't they?"). The Wachowskis' obsessive love of detail seems to extend even to their Oracle's costume: like the Sibyl/Oracle Michelangelo painted for the Sistine Chapel, their Oracle dresses in green and orange, and her cabinet features green countertops and orange doors.

The movie script describes the Oracle as "Sphinxlike," a reference to the mythological Greek creature famed for presenting riddles; this fierce creature had the body of a lion and the head of a woman. In Egyptian mythology, the Sphinx represented the sun god Re/Ra and once promised a prince that he would become pharaoh if he performed her a favor.

Greek references in *Reloaded* show the Wachowskis still up on their mythology. The steely character of Niobe, played by Jada Pinkett Smith, bears the name of the proud Theban whose pain turned her into an unfeeling rock, while the character of Persephone evokes the demigoddess carried off by Hades into the underworld (a situation that certainly reminds us of the Merovingian and his chateau) where her heart turned to ice. These references again add resonance to the film and help us understand a little better what the Wachowski brothers are trying to do.

But perhaps the clearest—and most profound—reference to the Greeks isn't a story of gods or goddesses at all.

PLATO AND THE ALLEGORY OF THE CAVE

The Greek philosopher Plato (428-348 B.C.E.) provides a clear source for the central idea behind *The Matrix*. He conceived of reality as a place divided between a world of ideas—a higher plane—and a world of forms—an inferior reflection of that plane. In Plato's vision of the universe, the world we experience is simply a shadow. In Book VII of *The Republic*, he created a powerful story, the Allegory of the Cave, to illustrate his ideas.

Plato called his readers to imagine living at the bottom of a long tunnel, in a cave where everyone was chained together facing a wall. Behind them, a fire projected light over a parapet, across which people, like puppetmasters, could carry artifacts—statues of men, say, or of animals. The chained viewers perceived these shadows as reality. Then Plato asked, How much inferior to the statues—or to the genuine creatures those statues represent—are those images? Yet from birth those chained humans experienced only these shadows, and however inferior or "unreal" their experience might seem, for them, it was the sum of existence.

The human beings in *The Matrix*, likewise, know no other experience; their lives consist of images projected into their brains. But for them these images are everything, and to tear them loose from this ersatz version of reality is to risk their destruction. In fact, Morpheus and the freedom fighters have made it a policy not to free people from the matrix past a certain age, because it is too difficult for them to make the adjustment to reality and keep their sanity.

Likewise, Plato wrote of the hazards facing those chained humans who might find release from their bonds. Even the dim light of the fire behind them would blind them. If they were compelled to make the journey out of the tunnel and into the upper world, they would find the light of the sun utterly ruinous.

In the film, Neo is carried up out of darkness (the dark pool beneath the bioenergy converters) into the blinding light emerging from the *Nebuchadnezzar*. And later, onboard ship, when Neo asks why his eyes hurt so badly, Morpheus responds, "Because you have never used them." Neo's escape from the matrix takes him into a world of higher reality, but the transition challenges him tremendously, and at first he reacts with anger and disbelief—just as Plato had prophesied. After Morpheus shows him the world as it is, he reacts angrily, violently, until he vomits and lapses into unconsciousness. The blinding nature of the real overwhelms him.

MORE THAN MEETS THE EYE

We can find myth everywhere in the world of *The Matrix*, from stories to character names to visual references. In *Reloaded*, we expand the repertoire, adding references to the Hindu goddess Kali, the epic hero Roland, the enchanted hammer of the Norse god of thunder, for crying out loud. It's an embarrassment of riches, a cornucopia of stories, all in service of a new myth. No wonder a fan of *The Matrix* told me these films have captured her attention and affection in a way no other film ever has: "It is a film that makes you think; you actually return home and want to read about the many ideas that emerge behind the action."

If a film can reignite a yearning for faith and the timeless questions of humanity, then we should engage the Wachowski brothers and their ideas. In the future we could judge great art (be it film, literature, or visual arts) by its ability to lead all of us to a place of dialogue and discussion.

On that scale, *The Matrix* is off the charts.

_9 //

_ MORPHEUS: A VOICE CRYING IN THE WILDERNESS _

Everything begins with choice.

MORPHEUS, in *Reloaded*

From the first time we see him, there's no question: this guy is *cool*.

Here is a man to be reckoned with. He seems to be the wisest human alive—and has a sense of style, to boot. Morpheus, as portrayed by Laurence Fishburne, is, as Richard Corliss put it, "every wise guide from literature, religion, movies, and comix."[1]

A JUMBLE OF HEROES

Fishburne describes his character's role in guiding the film's deliverer in this way: "It turns into a mentor-protégé thing. Morpheus is sort of part Obi-Wan Kenobi, part Darth Vader—if you splice the two together and add a little bit of Yoda."[2]

In Greek mythology, you'll recall, Morpheus is the god who rules over sleep and the dreams of all people. He could enter the dreams of anyone sleeping and take on any form. It is clear that this dark hero is powerful—but not powerful enough.

Morpheus comes from the same root word as *morph* (to bring objects together and join them as one), so it is fitting that this character represents a jumble of ideas and stereotypes: the White Rabbit, Batman, a prophet, any number of figures from myth and story. We're even invited to identify him with God. In the trinity of *The Matrix*, Morpheus represents God the Father. "You were more than just a leader to us," Tank says, "you were a father." And clearly, Neo, who trains under him and represents the Messiah, is his son.

But the most important of the associations that the Wachowskis create for Morpheus seems to be with the biblical figure of John the Baptist. In learning about this figure we can learn some important spiritual lessons.

JOHN AND MORPHEUS

Morpheus is an imposing figure in his own right, of course—wise, powerful in his faith. So was John. "No man born of woman" played a more important role than John, Jesus once said.[3] And both men shared a sort of infamy (although John clearly lacked Morpheus' sense of hygiene and fashion).

The Jewish historian, Josephus, has as much to say about John as he does about Jesus himself, a fact that declares the man's importance. French religious historian Mircea Eliade writes:

> He was a true prophet, illuminated, irascible, and vehement, in open rebellion against the Jewish political and religious hierarchies. Leader of a millenarianistic sect, John the Baptist announced the imminence of the Kingdom, but without claiming the title of its Messiah.[4]

The parallels to Morpheus seem clear: he likewise is a prophet in open rebellion against the system, and his "sect" certainly looks toward the end times—the destruction of the machines and the end of the world as they know it.

Like John, Morpheus does not claim to be the Messiah, but he knows he is coming and that he will recognize him when he sees him.

The gospel of Luke describes the scene when Jesus comes to John for baptism. "I'm the one who needs to be baptized," John protests, "not *you!*"[5] Morpheus, when greeted by the clearly impressed Neo for the first time, responds with similar awareness of the difference in their stations: "The honor is mine." Fishburne commented on this bit of dialogue: "I liken it to John the Baptist. 'No, I would rather be baptized by you.'"[6] Morpheus, much like John, baptizes Neo into the real world and pulls him up from the abyss to safety with his disciples on the *Nebuchadnezzar*.

When the Holy Spirit in the form of a dove descends on Jesus and declares him to be the Son of God, who can miss the clear marking-out that Jesus is special? In a similar way, Morpheus' continuing insistence that Neo is the One is part of that recognition in the *Matrix* films, and interestingly, he sends Trinity—who represents the Holy Spirit in the *Matrix* trilogy—to proclaim that set apartness to Neo.

Jesus did not fully begin his ministry until the powers-that-be (in those days, King Herod Antipas) imprisoned John. According to Josephus, Herod feared the influence and power John wielded and worried about a revolution. But whatever the reason for the prophet's imprisonment, it triggered Jesus' preaching.

Similarly, Morpheus' imprisonment prompts Neo's leap of faith, his assumption of responsibility, and the first clear proof of his power. Jesus and Neo both step up to the plate (or pick up their submachine guns—you choose the metaphor) when their powerful predecessor gets swept from the bases.

This crisis calls out the best in everyone. "On many levels," Fishburne says, "the movie is a lesson in faith. It's about belief in oneself, in the greatest good for everyone, in the human spirit—whatever you want to call it, whatever that quintessential faith is for you. It's about awakening. Whatever it is that leads you to it, whether it's somebody else's life being at risk, whether it's your need to seek someone out who can teach you greater truths or reveal to you your own truth by their example, whatever it is."[7]

In prison Herod had John beheaded—and the tight close-ups of Morpheus during his captivity may remind us of John's fate (as we similarly surmised about the beheaded Orpheus). John the Baptist, of course, was only human; he did not rise from the dead. Like Morpheus, he could confront evil but not defeat it. Only the One can do that; but without the prophet, there is no chosen One, and Morpheus serves this vital role in the world of *The Matrix*. Again, in the words of the actor who brings this character to life: "That's really where Morpheus plays an important part. It's not so much that the movie becomes about him. It becomes about faith, that epiphany that he talks about, 'One day you will understand like I understand.' It's like Martin Luther King, Jr. said, 'If you haven't found something for which you are prepared to die, then you aren't really living.' And when Neo gets to the place where he's prepared to forfeit his life in order to save someone else's, then he is truly alive."[8]

PREPARING THE PATH

History is littered with defining moments in which great people change the historical landscape of a nation or the world. But they do not act in a vacuum; someone sets the stage.

Be it Nelson Mandela, Mother Teresa, Billy Graham, Elie Wiesel, or Martin Luther King, Jr., they all had others who led them toward peace and justice. Sages have always offered counsel and inspired acts of self-sacrifice. In the hero's journey Joseph Campbell described, a mentor always helps the hero along his or her way. Everyone wants to be the savior, the center of attention. But it's more realistic—and just as important—for us to set our sights on challenging others to greatness.

The world is saved person by person, tiny step by tiny step.

_ 10 //

_ W A K E   U P ! _

Whadda I got to, whadda I got to do to wake ya up
To shake ya up, to break the structure up.

RAGE AGAINST THE MACHINE

Neo's wake-up call begins his spiritual awakening, starting him on a movement from drowsy drone to awakened One. We all need to follow a similar movement in life—which is one of the reasons *The Matrix* resonates so powerfully with viewers. Like most archetypal hero stories, Neo's story is also about us.

SLEEP AS A SYMBOL

We've already heard the warning cry from the Gnostic work called the *Apocalypse of John*: "Let him who hears wake from heavy sleep." Gnostic teachings typically identify sleep with ignorance and death.

But the Gnostics were hardly the only people in history to think of sleep as a symbol for blindness, for remaining sunk in a state of unenlightenment. In fact, as Mircea Eliade points out, ever since the adventures of *The Epic of Gilgamesh*, the world's first great work of literature, it has been known that conquering sleep—remaining awake—"constitutes the most difficult initiatory ordeal, for it seeks a transformation of the profane condition."[1]

Over thousands of years of human storytelling, we find ourselves drawn repeatedly to images of sleep and waking to explain to us the movement from a "profane condition"—that is, this earthly, material life—to a spiritual condition. We, too, want to wake up.

We are, to use the image from one of the Wachowskis' favorite anime cartoons, Ghosts trying to transcend our Shells. Or to use the language from another unlikely spiritual film, *Pulp Fiction*, we are the tyranny of evil men, trying real hard to be shepherds. Perhaps Paul the apostle said it best in his letter to the church in Ephesus: "Wake up from your sleep, climb out of your coffins; Christ will show you the light!"[2]

In any case, most people would agree that waking is good; we just don't always devote ourselves to it as we might. Perhaps a little reflection will give us some insight—and the impulse—we need to vigorously pursue genuine consciousness.

A TRADITIONAL AND BIBLICAL EQUATION

Shakespeare, in Hamlet's famous "To Be or Not to Be" soliloquy, used the traditional equation of "that sleep of death." The Bible frequently uses such an equation.

Often Scripture compares physical death to sleep—Lazarus sleeps in his tomb[3]—but more often it uses the idea of sleep to represent spiritual death or immaturity. The prophet Isaiah calls over and over, "Awake!" In the gospel of Mark, Jesus tells a story about the return of the master of the house and counsels his listeners to stay awake: "So stay at your post, watching. . . . You don't want him showing up unannounced, with you asleep on the job. I say it to you, and I'm saying it to all: Stay at your post.

Keep watch."[4]

In Mark's very next chapter we find one of the most poignant passages in the Bible. Jesus, awake and in anguish, asks his disciples to stay with him, to "keep vigil" as he wrestles with the greatest challenge of his life. Yet three times he returns to find them asleep. Once he asks Peter, "Can't you stick it out with me for a single hour? Stay alert, be in prayer, so you don't enter the danger zone without even knowing it." At last, the third time, he tells them simply, "Are you going to sleep all night? No—you've slept long enough. Time's up."[5]

Here we see a spiritual battle equivalent to *The Matrix*'s martial arts choreography. The Son of Man faces the knowledge that he is soon to die to redeem the world, and he asks his all-too-human friends to remain at his side, to give him some comfort—to take his back, if you will. But they are not up to the task. Mired in themselves and ignorant of a higher purpose, they sleep, until at last Jesus calls them to account. Now they will have to wake up, he says. The time has come for him to be taken from them—and they will have to stand on their own.

Likewise, the apostle Paul used the metaphors of sleeping and waking as part of his approach to drawing the early Christian churches into spiritual growth. In his letter to the Roman church, Paul sums up the importance of this spiritual awakening in the following words:

> Make sure that you don't get so absorbed and exhausted in taking care of all your day-by-day obligations that you lose track of the time and doze off, oblivious to God. The night is about over, dawn is about to break. Be up and awake to what God is doing! God is putting the finishing touches on the salvation work he began when we first believed.[6]

WAKING UP ANEW EVERY DAY

We can use the example of Neo to hearten us, because the salvation work we see in him comes about in fits and starts, in a series of awakenings. Waking up takes time and effort, and, as Morpheus says, *knowing* the path and *following* the path are two separate things.

When we first see Neo open his eyes, he is a seeker who hasn't found what he's looking for. He knows there is something more, something outside himself; he knows the world as it is can't satisfy him. But he doesn't know what will.

It's instructive to notice how many times in the film Neo "wakes up"— from sleep, from unconsciousness, or finally, at the end, from physical death. Waking up is a process. When we wake up, we follow the path whose outlines we know.

Elaine Pagels notes in *The Gnostic Gospels*, "Pursuing *gnosis* involves each person in a solitary, difficult process, as one struggles against internal resistance. They characterized this resistance to gnosis as the desire to sleep or to be drunk—that is, to remain unconscious."[7]

In thinking of these dual metaphors, it's interesting to think of Cypher, the only character in the movie associated with alcohol. He offers Neo a slug from his jug of homebrew aboard the ship and enjoys wine at his dinner with Agent Smith. Not that you can't enjoy wine with dinner! It's just clear that the Wachowskis employ alcohol as a symbol of Cypher's refusal to face the specter of spiritual change.

We use anything at our fingertips as a means to slumber. Alcohol numbs. Television anesthetizes. Work fills the hours of the day so that we may ignore our realities. And with what do the majority of us fill our lives? Alcohol, television, work . . . and sleep.

The prophet Isaiah spoke of men like Cypher who would choose blindness over sight, and who, once having been awakened, are numbed again by ignorance. It would seem the Wachowski brothers had the prophet's warning in the back of their minds as they shot the poignant scene where Cypher savors filet mignon—at least, that is what he wants to believe:

> Like a hungry man dreaming he's eating steak
>> and wakes up hungry as ever,
> Like a thirsty woman dreaming she's drinking iced tea
>> and wakes up thirsty as ever,
> So that mob of nations at war against Mount Zion
>> will wake up and find they haven't shot an arrow,
>> haven't killed a single soul.[8]

Cypher abandons his faith for ease. Like many of us, he chooses to forfeit the battle—a battle that, with Neo, he was destined to win.

THE DIFFERENCE BETWEEN AWAKE AND BUSY

Like Neo, we, too, are waking up. We are recognizing that the corporate scurrying so many of us endure mirrors the meaningless, illusory world of hurry and bustle inside the matrix—as meaningless as the blather spouted by Neo's superior at Metacortex. We mistake being busy for being awake, and being still, or reflective, for being asleep.

It's important here to think about the mystics, monks, and reflective ones of the world. Or think of Neo and Morpheus, motionless in their chairs aboard the *Nebuchadnezzar*, their bodies in repose but their minds seeking and finding. It's an interesting—and particularly important—paradox for us to remember in these oh-so-busy days of the new millennium. Remember the matrix-training program in which Neo gets banged into by business lemmings as he tries to walk down the sidewalk. It's at that point Morpheus calls for a stop—and in the reflective moment, learning takes place.

Jesus calls all of us to this space of contemplation and holy engagement. "Here's what I want you to do," he says. "Find a quiet, secluded place so you won't be tempted to role-play before God. Just be there as simply and honestly as you can manage. The focus will shift from you to God, and you will begin to sense his grace."[9]

There is much for us to learn. We, too, are called to wake up. We, too, must blunder our way forward from waking to waking, hoping to become spiritually stronger with each new awakening. Like the disciples, we need to learn to keep our eyes open, to walk with Jesus just a little farther. Like the Roman church to whom Paul wrote, we need to make sure we don't sink so deeply in the everyday that we lose sight of what is truly important: the spiritual life and our walking of that path. And like Neo, we need to learn the difference between sleep and waking up to all the possibilities available on the path.

YOU REAP WHAT YOU SOW

The first movie closes with Rage Against the Machine's "Wake Up," a line from which reminds us, "What you reap is what you sow." If we want to reap wakefulness, then it's necessary to sow it.

Here's hoping we start now.

_ 11 //

_ W A L K I N G   T H E   P A T H _

I just wish I knew what I'm supposed to do.

NEO, in *Reloaded*

In the first *Matrix* film, Neo had to reach up to one great act of faith. In retrospect, it seems relatively simple: to accept the path. His destiny—to be "the One"—is no better than any of ours, merely different.

Throughout *The Matrix: Reloaded*, we're treated to an assortment of questions and comments on fate and free will, on following the path, on the possibility of prophecy coming true. Many of these new ideas complicate—or even argue against—those presented in the original film.

We could scratch our heads and decide it's too hard to puzzle out a response to all these possibilities. We could dig in our heels and say we're sticking with the old story and forget what we see going on around us. Or we could remember the lesson of the *Matrix* films we've seen so many times before: like our postmodern world, the films burst with different histories, different stories, different philosophies, and different faiths, and it is our responsibility as living, breathing, aware human beings to find the things that help us to make sense of our lives.

FINDING THE PATH VERSUS WALKING IT

The Matrix emphasizes acceptance as the central element of faith. There is a path.

Repeatedly Trinity declares her belief that Neo is the One prophesied, the incarnation of a powerful being who lived outside the power of the matrix. She proclaims her faith to Neo at the beginning of the film, to the Oracle midway through, and to Morpheus throughout. And for Neo as a character—and for us as viewers—this acceptance, the claiming of this story, feels both powerful and moving.

We've seen how Neo's growth and development in the first film parallels that of many spiritual traditions, how it fits the archetypal hero's journey. Keanu Reeves says, "The first film was about the birth of a hero; the second and third are the life of that hero."[1] And life has a way of complicating things.

Our own introduction to a life of faith, like that of Neo, revolves around seeing ourselves in a new way: redeemed, transformed. Once we grasp our new identity, we become ready to walk the path of faith.

In the first film, Morpheus serves in the role of visionary, the John the Baptist figure predicting the way to come. His faith in Neo and in the path remain so absolute that we urge Neo to believe; we believe, ourselves. But, as in life, the sequels complicate and even contradict what we think we know about life.

Morpheus and Neo confront ideas in the sequels that suggest they may have been wrong about fate and the future. And what they do with these reversals brings us some illumination as well.

REVERSALS AND SURPRISES

Dialogue in *The Matrix* describes the Oracle as "one of us" who had been with the resistance from the beginning. In the sequels, Neo realizes that she is a program, part of the matrix; the Architect of the matrix calls her the Mother of the program.

Neo wonders if he can trust her when he discovers she is a product of code. In her typically Oraclean way, she tells him that ultimately, he has to make up his own mind about what to believe. And she insists, "We're all here to do what we're all here to do."

That line is echoed throughout the film, by both machines and by people. We all serve a function; we're here to keep plugging along; we have a role that belongs to us alone. Here we confront the nature of the path and our dependence on dream, prophecy, or wishful thinking.

Morpheus made promises to Neo (and to us). Neo would save the world from the machines. Zion would be safe. But as we come to the end of *Reloaded* and look forward to the third film, much of what we thought we knew has fallen into ruins. Morpheus has lost his ship, and in seeing the destruction of the *Nebuchadnezzar*, he paraphrases a ruler from the fourth chapter of Daniel: "I have dreamed a dream." Morpheus believed in the prophecy—which the Architect of the matrix has said is false, a part of a larger, insidious plan. Is the prophecy true or is it another form of manipulation?

As Richard Corliss asks, "Were Morpheus and his band the only realists, or were they the victims of a monstrous delusion?"[2]

FAITH IN THE FACE OF ADVERSITY

Good news is coming, even if hard times are on the way. We know from experience—and from the lives of those who have walked close to God—that faith doesn't guarantee an easy life.

Consider the deprivation and desolation of Job. Look at the Hebrew prophet Hosea, whose unfaithful wife broke his heart. Recall the tragic, violent end of John the Baptist.

Lots of people recognize the path but refuse to follow it. The rich young ruler, who asked Jesus what he needed to do to be saved, correctly identified the path but chose not to enter it. Recognizing the path is only the first step, what Keanu Reeves described as the birth of a hero. Remaining faithful to that path—even when it doesn't seem to lead anywhere, or worse, seems to head into a deep, dark forest—is a good deal harder.

In the story of Nebuchadnezzar, the mad king of Babylon, we find hope. One night the king dreamed of exile and madness. He sought out Daniel to explain the dream, and the prophet warned Nebuchadnezzar that until he recognized the authority and fullness of God, he would lose both himself and his kingdom. By the end of the story, Nebuchadnezzar learned the lesson and God allowed him to return to himself. At last he could speak words that seem to illuminate the problems of *Reloaded*: "His miracles are staggering, his wonders are surprising. His kingdom lasts and lasts, his sovereign rule goes on forever."[3] Did he feel this way in his darkest days? Not likely. But in the fullness of time, Nebuchadnezzar looked back down the path and saw how the briars, tangles, and missteps had at last led to joy.

In a similar way, Morpheus may feel shaken in his faith and in his person by the events of *Reloaded*, but the Nebuchadnezzar story suggests how God leads us into a new, better relationship.

A CHOICE OF DOORS

Neo, however, remains our focus, since his rising and advancement so echo our own. His choices at the end of *Reloaded* carry as much power as any spiritual lessons from the first film.

When confronted by the Architect, Neo could react in any number of ways, but ultimately everything gets pared down to one choice: this door or that one? One asks Neo to renounce his path, to give up his plan to bring complete freedom to humankind, in exchange for the survival of a few free humans. The other offers him the impossible chance to save the life of Trinity, although the attempt will bring certain destruction to Zion.

The importance of dreams, prophecy, and predictions is highlighted in his choice. The movie begins with Neo's dream of Trinity's death and he wrestles with that terrible vision throughout the film. If he sees it, is it predestined? What are his possible choices? And in arguing with the Oracle, we see his discomfort with the questions of predestination and free will. "You've already made [the choice]," the Oracle tells him. "You're here to try to understand why you made it."

Her declaration doesn't help—and it goes against everything we want to believe. We want control. The question really comes down to this: do my choices make a difference? Is it worth continuing on a path even when I don't see results? Even when things go horribly wrong?

Reloaded has an answer to these questions. The Architect has told Neo that he cannot rescue Trinity. It is impossible. Neo has seen her fall to her death. But motivated by his love for her—like the love of Christ for his bride, the church—Neo willingly makes the attempt. He doesn't know what will happen. It seems impossible, according to everything he knows.

But one choice remains true to the path he has chosen, and the other renounces it. More to the point, one path chooses hope over despair or resignation. The Architect tells Neo, "Hope. It is the quintessential human delusion, simultaneously the source of your greatest strength and your greatest weakness." Perhaps, to a machine, love, hope, and faith in the future seem like weaknesses. But not to us.

By choosing to remain faithful to his path, Neo does the impossible, answers the naysayers, and flabbergasts the prophets. Not only does Neo snatch up Trinity a moment before she hits the ground, but when she dies from her wound, he becomes for her what she was for him at the end of *The Matrix*: a voice of hope who refuses to give up. "Trinity," he tells her, "I know you can hear me. I'm not letting go." He loves her too much.

The prophecies were wrong; the prophecies were right. The Oracle was a rebel; the Oracle was a machine. The Source would bring victory; the Source was another machine ploy, part of the ongoing plan.

Time will tell which of these will prove right or wrong, which are lies from the Architect. But ultimately it doesn't matter. *Reloaded* brings another message of faith, a message not of understanding, but of doing: *Follow the path.*

WE ARE LOVED

God has given each of us certain things to do in this world. The story of the hero's journey tells us that we will face problems along the way, that we will have to leave behind the things we know — but that what we learn will not only save us but help save others.

Neo's journey likewise teaches us the importance of faithfulness, the power of love, and the possibilities before us. However difficult the road ahead may prove to be, it's good to be reminded that we are loved—and that there is One who will never let us go.

_ 12 //

_ TRINITY: THE FEMALE FACE OF GOD _

*I wish to show you Truth herself; for I have brought her down from above,
so that you may see her without a veil, and understand her beauty.*

IRENAEUS, *Libros Quinque Adversus Haereses I.14.3*

Who can forget the first time they saw Trinity in *The Matrix*? This beautiful woman, surprised by two units of police officers, puts her hands up—and then proceeds to defy gravity by putting the rest of herself up, hanging in the air in the first recorded use of the now-familiar "bullet time." In the sequence that follows, she runs up the wall of the hotel room, awes pursuing cops by leaping across an impossible space, and then flies across a street and through a window.

Clearly, this is no retiring female.

And just as clearly, she is no secondary character. We have heard her arguing with Cypher in the first moments of the film as he declares, "We'll kill him [Neo]"; now she becomes the first character we follow. Trinity—as character and symbol—is central to the *Matrix* films.

MORE THAN A SINGLE FIGURE

Actor Joe Pantoliano has laid out some possible biblical correspondences to characters in the *Matrix* films. He says that his character, Cypher, could be viewed as a Judas figure. Morpheus, as we've seen, could be considered a John the Baptist analogue. And one could read Trinity as Mary Magdalene. But Trinity represents much more than this single figure from the Gospel accounts.

In fact, on one level, Trinity is God herself. Her name alone reminds us of this function. If Morpheus represents the Father and Neo the Son, then Trinity must represent the third face of the Godhead: the Spirit, the force acting in the world.

This idea of the Spirit of God as feminine is not unusual: the Hebrew idea of God's Spirit—the Spirit who inhabited the Holy of Holies in the temple—found its place in the Bible through a feminine word, *ruah*. The Hebrews also personified Wisdom (*hokma*, in the Hebrew, or *sophia*, as the Greeks would have it) as a feminine mediator between God and man. Mircea Eliade writes, "Certain schools of wisdom promoted *hokma* to the rank of supreme authority, as mediatrix of the Revelation."[1] This would certainly describe Trinity, who serves as the mediatrix of the revelation in *The Matrix*. In this vein, consider the following lines about Lady Wisdom in the book of Proverbs:

> You can find me on Righteous Road—that's where I walk—
> > at the intersection of Justice Avenue,
> Handing out life to those who love me,
> > filling their arms with life. . . .
> God sovereignly made me—the first, the basic—
> > before he did anything else. . . .
> When you find me, you find life, real life.[2]

In *The Matrix*, Trinity brings Neo to "real life," the life of the world outside the matrix. And when Neo dies, it is Trinity who "hands out life" to him, bringing him back from death. In this way, Trinity echoes her function as the Christian Holy Spirit, or Paraclete, the third member of the Trinity. In this role as the Breath of God, the Holy Spirit brought Jesus back to life; and so it is that Trinity breathes life back into Neo as she brings her face to his and kisses him.

The first public appearance of the Holy Spirit in the Gospels comes when the dove settles on Jesus during his baptism and God identifies him as "my son, in whom I am well pleased."[3] The Holy Spirit functions here as a herald, bringing news of chosen-ness to Jesus and to those who witness the event.

This is exactly the role played by Trinity in the early part of *The Matrix*. She is the first of the forces of Zion to appear to Neo, the first to tell him that he is something special, something set apart. Interestingly, she tells him when she first meets him in person that she understands what he wants and what he seeks because she and he are alike; she used to seek the same thing. (And who would be more alike than two parts of the Godhead?)

Gnostic Visions of God

As we consider some Gnostic versions of Christianity, so important to the Wachowski brothers' conception of the *Matrix* films, we can clearly see the idea of God as a female. Some Gnostic texts speak of a Divine Mother; more interesting, perhaps, for our purposes, are texts that consider the Holy Spirit as female.

The *Apochryphon of John* describes a mystic vision that John received after the Crucifixion, a vision of the Trinity: God the Father, God the Mother, God the Son. The *Gospel to the Hebrews* has Jesus speak of his Mother, the

Spirit. The *Gospel of Thomas* contrasts Jesus' earthly mother and father with "his divine Father—the Father of Truth—and his divine Mother, the Holy Spirit."[4]

In the Gnostic tradition, God has plenty of room for the feminine, something often missing from more mainstream Christianity. As Elaine Pagels noted, by 200 C.E., "Virtually all the feminine imagery for God had disappeared from orthodox Christian tradition."[5] So Trinity reminds us of an alternative set of beliefs. Trinity is a version of the beautiful, wise—and, let's face it, powerful—female face of the divine.

SET ASIDE FOR A SPECIAL RELATIONSHIP

Besides Trinity's characterization as the herald/messenger/Holy Spirit in the films, she serves other key roles. For one, she is an indispensable fellow traveler. Her destiny gets caught up in Neo's because of the Oracle's prophecies, and because her own destiny cannot be completed without him. She is also helper and sidekick.

When Neo decides to return to the matrix to rescue Morpheus from the Agents, Trinity tells him she is going with him. When he tries to refuse, she tells him in no uncertain terms that if he doesn't like it, "I believe you can go to hell." (In another ancient text, *The Harrowing of Hell*, Jesus descends to hell to confront Satan; the Holy Spirit brings him out when she brings him back to life. Without the Holy Spirit—as Neo without Trinity—Christ cannot complete his appointed task to redeem the world.)

Perhaps most important is the love connection between Trinity and Neo. In symbolic terms, perhaps we could think of their physical love as a spiritual or mystical bond, or as a combination of male and female aspects of

God that together represent the totality of experience.

But frankly, we can also think of it strictly in generic terms: this is a Hollywood movie, after all, which means we need a love story. As elsewhere in the *Matrix* films, we should never push comparisons so far that they lose their value. Trinity can simultaneously be *ruah*, and Wisdom, and Holy Spirit, and the female love interest, and one wicked kung fu babe. One reading doesn't have to preclude the others. Let's find our meanings where we can.

_13 //

_ I K N O W K U N G F U _

You do not truly know someone until you fight them.

S E R A P H , in *Reloaded*

If you were to ask a fan whether he or she watches the *Matrix* films for the spiritual and philosophical insights or for the action, you'd likely get some strange looks.

Hey, those glares would probably suggest, *if you want religion or philosophy, go to a Bible study, pick up a volume of Aristotle, or join a chat room.* We generally don't go to Hollywood films for insight—but it's a nice serendipity when we can find some amid the combat training and mind-blowing special effects.

On the Firing Range

The *Matrix* trilogy offers a popular film package with a sugar-coated pill inside. There we find kernels of truth within a hard-action capsule.

Why all the cinematic fireworks? The Wachowski brothers wanted people to actually *watch* their film. They also wanted to pay homage to dramatic and comic action that they themselves love—therefore, action comprises a significant part of the *Matrix* corpus. It's important to note, though, that the films spend more time in philosophical discussion than on the firing range.

All the same, it's the wild, violent action that most people remember when they think of the movies. And since we're making a case for the films as carriers of meaning, especially regarding issues of religion and spirituality, we have to account for the violence as well.

We might as well face it: whether we're talking about Buddhism or Christianity, the use of violence to solve problems raises new problems for interpretation. And the addition of the video game, *Enter the Matrix*—a game that producer Joel Silver calls an integral part of the *Matrix* universe and which features an incredible investment in cast and special effects, as well as martial arts action choreographed by Yuen Wo Ping—makes it clear that violence comprises an integral part of the *Matrix* universe.

So again we need to take a closer look and think more deeply about precedents, images, symbols, and context. What can *The Matrix* possibly have to tell us about faith and spirit through the medium of violence?

SPIRITUAL WARFARE, RENDERED DRAMATICALLY

We could perhaps make a defense for the films by claiming that they depict spiritual warfare, rendered dramatically. Evangelical Christians notwithstanding, who wants to see a movie about people *praying* for good to prevail?

For every good Christian kid who ever sat in church imagining what he would do to Satan if he could get him in his crosshairs, the idea of violence in spiritual battle seems not so far-fetched. In some ways, we can all support this idea.

Faith and enlightenment clearly get measured in *The Matrix* by martial prowess. Neo's first great task—to overcome the Agents—is presented as a threshold crossing. "They are guarding all the exits," Morpheus says. The enemies hold all the keys. They must be defeated—and given the laws of the world Neo must enter to defeat them, Morpheus is not talking about checkers. So Neo must destroy Agent Smith in battle, or the quest to free humanity will fail and the rest of the world will live and die unenlightened, in thrall to the machines.

We could also argue that the world of *The Matrix* is unreal—a dream world, as Morpheus calls it. We know that we are meant to identify the matrix with a state of oblivion or unenlightened being. The Gnostic *Gospel of Truth* even seems to echo Neo's nightmare experiences in the matrix and the training programs that replicate it for him:

> Either there is a place to which they are fleeing, or, without strength, they come from having chased after others, or they are involved in striking blows, or they are receiving blows themselves, or they have fallen from high places, or they take off into the air though they do not have wings.
>
> . . . When those who are going through all these things wake up, they see nothing, for they are nothing. Such is the way of those who have cast ignorance aside as sleep, leaving its works behind him like a dream in the night. . . . This is the way everyone has acted, as though asleep at the time when he was ignorant. And this is the way he has come to knowledge, as if he has awakened.[1]

Still, even though we can make a case for the action as a dream, or as merely emblematic of spiritual warfare, the cinematic reality feels so compelling, so powerful, that it remains troublesome. And not only do we witness the violence of the extended gunfights and martial arts battles; people hooked up to the matrix clearly die in these dream-battles. So we remember that those who die in the matrix die in reality. The spirit cannot survive without the body. So salvation comes with a real price. A high price.

What are we to do with all of this?

THE PORNOGRAPHY OF VIOLENCE?

Despite the powerful meta-story and eye-popping special effects, some viewers walked out of theaters disgusted by this blockbuster hit. Violence exploded in the "real world" just weeks after the film's Easter release, forcing us to examine the factors that led to this brutality.

Prior to 9-11, the greatest horror imaginable was a massacre of our children by other children. The world seemed to change overnight when blood flowed in a suburban high school now known to the world simply as Columbine. Who or what was to blame? The disenfranchisement caused by schoolyard bullies? Senseless violence acted out in graphic video games? Explicit scenes splashed on the Internet? The desire to be known, the incredible media attention given to earlier schoolyard shootings? The influence of films like *The Matrix*? If they led us to the disaster at Columbine, then the future appears very bleak indeed.

In April of 1999, the on-screen depiction of Neo and Trinity—fully clad in long, leather coats and storming a federal building in a torrential downpour of gunfire—brought no comfort. In fact, it felt nothing but gut wrenching. Because on April 20, 1999, Eric Harris and Dylan Klebold stormed their classrooms in Littleton, Colorado, clad in trench coats. With guns blazing, they killed twelve students, one teacher, and wounded twenty others. Surviving students described a bloodbath in a place American families had believed to be safe. This was a nightmare in the heart of our homeland, and we went searching for someone to blame.

Warner Brothers took some significant hits from conservatives and Hollywood pundits. Vice President Al Gore, who had earlier said he liked the movie, changed his tune, and the Archbishop of the Denver Diocese, Charles Chaput, said that if Harris and Klebold saw the film, its depiction of violence "certainly didn't deter them."[2] Richard Corliss summed up the furor in his *Time* article, "Unlocking The Matrix." He said the film caught the "wrathful attention of moral watchdogs" because it appeared as if Harris and Klebold "had seen the film"—although he deftly pointed out, so did "15 million people who didn't kill anyone."[3]

Other things also give us pause. The Agents in the film describe Morpheus and his crew as "terrorists," a word that carried a different, less personal meaning in the late 1990s. In 2003, we are no strangers to terror. The warnings greet us with every newspaper, political talk show, or trip to the airport.

So will the public reject *Reloaded* and *Revolutions* because of our increased sensitivity to violence?

Not likely.

Jesus the Revolutionary

Many of us forget the extent to which Jesus was born into occupied territory. And yet, trying to imagine the life of Christ without taking into account the Roman conquest is unthinkable.

Former priest and devout Catholic James Carroll argues, "The origins of the Jesus movement, Christianity, cannot be understood apart from the century-long Roman war against the Jews, albeit a war punctuated by occasional acts of Jewish rebellion. . . . Jesus and his movement were born in the shadow of what would stand as the most grievous violence against the Jewish people until Hitler's attempt at a Final Solution."[4]

Jesus, like Neo in *The Matrix*, entered the story as a member of a conquered race, into a land ruled by a tyrannical power that had to be overthrown if his people were ever to be truly free. This helps explain the expectations of the Jews for their Messiah: that he would liberate them from tyranny. In Jewish thought, it was impossible to separate things of this world from spiritual things. So why *wouldn't* a Messiah care about temporal matters? It also explains why some Jews refused to accept Jesus as the Messiah. He preached the kingdom of God within each person, not as a place on a map, a place free of Roman oppression—and such a vision simply didn't match their hopes or expectations.

Jesus came to earth primarily to inaugurate a final fulfillment of prophecy, to provide an ultimate example of holiness, and to fully incarnate God's love. He didn't come to stir up trouble against local rulers.

A TROUBLING INCIDENT

Still, there's that disturbing incident in the temple. Remember? Jesus as Rambo, turning over tables and whipping money-changers.

This event unsettles and, in some ways, puzzles us. Jesus, as a Jew, knew that the merchants he terrorized served a function. Pilgrims needed to buy a pigeon to perform a sacrifice, or they might need to change their money into the proper local currency to purchase another sacrificial animal.

Theologians have read this event in different ways; some have connected it to a revolutionary attack against the temple and what it represented—a symbol of a corrupt society, say some, or a way of worship that had become overly commercialized, say others. Some say Jesus objected to the overly ornate (and extremely Hellenized) temple of Herod, who had become "king of the Jews" by decree of the Romans. Perhaps Jesus was opening up the temple so all could enter; after Jesus tossed over the tables and tossed out the merchants, the gospel of Matthew tells us, "Now there was room for the blind and crippled to get in. They came to Jesus and he healed them."[5]

Without question, Jesus' temple behavior grew violent (this chapter in Matthew calls it "outrageous," describes Jesus as "fed up," and includes the disturbing incident of the fig tree that Jesus withered because it produced no fruit for him to eat). We don't normally think of Jesus as destructive or willingly killing anything, even plant life. But Jesus used this act of destruction as a teaching moment, describing faith's power to do miracles and move mountains: "You'll not only do minor feats like I did to the fig tree, but also triumph over huge obstacles."[6]

Like defeat Agents, perhaps?

Jujitsu for Jesus

Even though Jesus, and Christian thinkers since, advocated peace, he seems to have leaned toward action when it seemed necessary to create a better, more peaceful world, a world where people could come to him or grow in their faith.

This brings us to the dilemma of *The Matrix*. Is it acceptable to use force to free the people hooked up to the matrix, even to kill some of those who resist?

The ranks of history are not empty of holy people who resorted to violence. Often, it's the other way around. For every holy Shaolin monk trained in martial arts who uses his abilities to protect the helpless, we have scores of Crusader knights and Islamic jihadists killing enemies in the name of their faith. Far too many people over the ages have felt so sure they were right that they charged into battle, confident that God rode on their side. Sometimes these battles—such as the wars of the Reformation and Counter-Reformation—erupted over something not much more important than what particular kind of Christian message you believed. In the Middle Ages, soldiers who embarked on the Albigensian Crusade felt unsure how to tell the difference between "good" Christians and "bad." A representative of Pope Innocent told them, "Kill them all. God will know his own."

The *Matrix* films examine this kind of surety—I'm right and everyone else is wrong. Morpheus, Neo, and the others fight what we might call a "just" or "righteous" war. The machines are literally sucking the life out of their oppressed people, and they're not likely to stop because of acts of civil disobedience or peace meetings in Switzerland. The pacifist, Martin Luther King, Jr., knew that freedom must be demanded, that oppressors never voluntarily hand over power to the oppressed.

King's approach—and ours, generally—has been to hope for peaceful solutions to difficult problems. But given that civil disobedience and pacifism provide no solutions to the tyranny of the machines in *The Matrix* (can you imagine the "copper-tops" in their goop-filled cribs going on strike?), we can accept that only violence will overthrow them. In the *Matrix* films,

Neo and the others take individual human lives—humans who oppose the Zionists, or bodies "possessed" by Agents. This seems an acceptable—if regrettable—use of violence. It comes in self-defense, after all. If they don't take up arms, they will be killed themselves, and Zion will be destroyed.

But it should remain a troubling thing. We should never feel so sure of our righteousness—our rightness—that we choose violence over other solutions until all other solutions fail.

A Final Lesson

The *Matrix* films seem ever more relevant in a world that grows ever more troubling. We find ourselves asking the same kinds of questions about freeing the oppressed in Iraq, Iran, or North Korea. We are challenged to examine our motives. If they are to free the captives, then we should move swiftly; if they are to squelch our enemy or seek selfish gain, it is time to find other solutions.

And we must consider Jesus' reaction when Peter tries to defend him against the temple soldiers at the betrayal: "All who use swords are destroyed by swords," he declared. "Don't you realize that I am able right now to call to my Father, and twelve companies—more, if I want them—of fighting angels would be here, battle-ready?"[7] It almost sounds like a scene from *The Matrix*. And Peter, no doubt, would eagerly order them up to save Jesus. But imagine the result—the carnage, the loss of life . . . and the loss of human redemption.

Sure, it *would* have been a cool (if short) battle. But Jesus put people first. And for him, the cost of such a battle was just too high.

_14 //

_ E N S L A V E D   T O   C R E A T I O N _

Whenever I hear anyone arguing for slavery,
I feel a strong impulse to see it tried on him personally.

ABRAHAM LINCOLN

The story lines of the three *Matrix* films offer a singular vision: that all mankind should be free, liberated from restrictive or bigoted thinking, totalitarian regimes, or addictive substances. So far in this book we've heard the call to wake up and seen the challenge of taking a leap of faith. These are necessary components to freeing ourselves—and possibly our world—from bondage and oppression.

In the first film, Morpheus explains to Neo that the secret he is discovering will not go away. Neo is a slave. He does not know who owns him or how he has been captured, but he knows he is somehow incomplete. He seeks that which would make him free.

But freedom is a hard thing to gain; it's more than just a word on a page, a flag flapping in a breeze, a decision to do better or seek the right. Bondage ensnares our minds and we live continuously under its power. We long to live in ignorance of our state, but even in our denial, some part of us knows the truth.

Neo remembers being captured by the Agents and implanted with an intelligent organism that will track his movements. Yet he seeks to bury these facts in his subconscious. When his liberators expose the predator hiding in his belly, he exclaims, "That thing's real?"

Yes, Neo. And so are your worst fears.

A WORLD IN CHAINS

The Christian Scriptures paint a world in which we all are slaves. The question is simple: Who or what will *you* serve? Or put another way, who or what owns your soul? Is it sex, money, power and prestige, the desire to be in control?

As Christ said, "No one can serve two masters."[1] A murderer-turned-apostle made his loyalties clear: "I, Paul, am a devoted slave of Jesus Christ on assignment, authorized as an apostle to proclaim God's words and acts."[2]

So if we remain enslaved to something — even the ideal of our own personal freedom can become a form of slavery — then to what should we pledge our allegiance? Should the billions freed from the powers of the matrix and the machines pledge their loyalties to Neo? Can we choose to give ourselves to a cause, faith, or belief that can change the world for the better? Morpheus says that many people are not *ready*, and Cypher proves that some are not *willing*, to trade their form of slavery for truth. And yet, as Morpheus reminds us in *Reloaded*, there are things worth living — and dying — for.

A SKELETON IN THE CLOSET

For many, the quest to gain control of others becomes a new master; we can be enslaved by our desire to enslave. Oppression is humanity's chink in the armor, the skeleton in our collective closets—and no group of people remains innocent.

Although history indicts us all, our memories fade quickly. The successors to Christians devoured by lions for sport and persecuted by the Roman Empire for worshiping strange gods in turn showed brutal intolerance when Christianity became the state religion. Similarly, the Puritans who fled England to gain religious freedom denied that same religious freedom to those in the Massachusetts Bay Colony who didn't think as they did. American Southerners in the nineteenth century did not invent slavery; they only perfected its hypocrisy. They sang the virtues of freedom and formed their Methodist and Baptist denominations around their defense of owning fellow humans.

And consider the Jews, persecuted across the centuries. Hitler almost destroyed European Jewry in the 1930s and 1940s through his Final Solution, his busy poison gas facilities and concentration camps snuffing out millions of lives. So the survivors gained their own homeland, Israel, in 1948   and after achieving a measure of security against their neighbors, they now intern the Palestinians who used to occupy Israel/Palestine, controlling their daily movements to and from their West Bank ghettos. As the courageous Jewish theologian Marc Ellis has argued throughout his career, if the price of being Chosen is to become an agent of injustice, then something terribly wrong has happened to the call, some priorities have become horribly skewed.

Why is it that the oppressed, when freed, so often begin to oppress others?

The Garden of Eden tells the story of man's quest to be like God; lording over another seems a natural way to demonstrate godlike power. Thus our record of slavery, economic oppression, and war.

OBSERVING LIFE THROUGH THE NEBUCHADNEZZAR

The name of Morpheus' ship, the *Nebuchadnezzar*, provides us with a clear signal to look at the question of oppression, of opposition to oppression, and of ways to live in an imperfect world without becoming enslaved by it.

Nebuchadnezzar was undoubtedly the most eccentric and dominant king of ancient Babylon. He destroyed Israel in 586 B.C.E., raiding the temple as his armies killed and destroyed everything in their path. Only a remnant survived. A small group of Jews who escaped was sold into slavery or made to serve the king. Among the last few were Daniel, Shadrach, Meshach, and Abednego, a group of teenage boys recognized as intelligent, handsome, and without physical defect.

The king's chief official selected this trio for training in an elite school for future Babylonian leaders. These adolescent captives were brought to the center of world power (ironically, we would call the descendants of this empire "Iraqis"), where they were to be brainwashed into adopting the religion, values, and diet of their captors. How could these boys, the last hope for Israel, remain faithful to their people and their God in a culture that stood in complete opposition to their heritage? How could they remain forces for the good? In the words of Christ, they must live in the world without becoming a product of the world.

Each of them had to take a stand and face terrible dangers. Shadrach, Meshach, and Abednego refused to bow down to a golden statue of the king erected expressly for that purpose. Even when threatened with capital punishment, they stuck to their guns. As a result, they were sentenced to burn to death in a superheated furnace. But God honored their choice and an angel came to protect them in the flames. Because they chose to sacrifice their lives in order to do what was right, they found a safe haven even in the blast furnace.

The same is true of the *Nebuchadnezzar's* futuristic crew inside their hi-tech haven. They must descend into the matrix and work as forces of liberation and freedom from the inside—*in* that world, but not *of* it.

This essential element of the story—incarnation—provides a model of Christian redemption, salvation, and freedom. Sadly, many people of faith have developed a sort of amnesia when it comes to incarnational theology. Thankfully, leaders like Archbishop Desmond Tutu do their best to awaken us from such forgetfulness. Our faith is truly incarnational—in danger and in sanctuary, in churches, parliaments, and on street corners. God wants to work through each of us in the world, and through us he pursues his goals of justice and peace.

It is not about what you know; it is about how you live. Even if Neo knew and accepted fully his destiny as the One, it wouldn't matter unless he began to live it. Faith without action is dead.

Christ made it clear how we could identify those who follow him: "They will love one another."[3] In a similar way, Neo and his revolutionary disciples demonstrate their belief in justice by living in harm's way so that all may be free. Again, we remember the words of Christ: no greater love can be imagined than that a person should lay down his life for another.[4] In *The Matrix*, the Oracle tells Neo that Morpheus believes in him so completely that he is willing to risk his life; then she tells Neo that he will have to decide who will live. Neo puts his own life on the line, does indeed end up losing it, but ultimately gains so much more.

A living faith calls all of us to live in the culture and avoid the seclusion of religion, what John Milton referred to as "cloistered virtue." It's unsafe out there—but we still have this much control over things even in a world enslaved: we can decide how we will live and die, and we can choose to live rightly.

STANDING FOR TRUTH IN HOSTILE PLACES

Daniel, the Jewish teen whose life we just recalled, could be a guide for all of us. He provides a perfect picture of how to stand for truth even while immersed in a hostile religious culture.

Young Daniel earned a perfect 4.0 in the school of Babylon. The king considered him ten times wiser than the sages who taught him. Daniel even took the Babylonian name Belteshazzar, yet he refused to defile the Most High God by eating unclean food, bowing to idols, or ceasing his regular times of prayer. Doing right meant taking a stand and running a risk. Daniel's insistence on continuing to pray to God—and not to the king—put him in grave danger. He received a death sentence and found himself tossed into a den of ravenous lions. Yet once more God sent an angel to protect his faithful follower and save him from certain death.

Morpheus' ship, the *Nebuchadnezzar*, likewise provided a place of safety for Neo. In its friendly confines he felt embraced by a community, was trained for his future endeavors, and found solace while preparing for the battle that awaited him.

At the center of this ship—the nuclear reactor, the power source, if you will—is a small identifying plaque: Mark III no. 11. Most critics have noted this as yet another reference to Neo's role as the savior: Mark 3:11 identifies Jesus as the Son of God. But the third chapter of Mark's gospel also frames the space that this vessel would play for the Neo-Christ and his journey to save mankind:

> Jesus went off with his disciples to the sea to get away. But a huge crowd from Galilee trailed after them—also from Judea, Jerusalem, Idumea, across the Jordan, and around Tyre and Sidon—swarms of people who had heard the reports and had come to see for themselves. He told his disciples to get a boat ready so he wouldn't be trampled by the crowd. He had healed many people, and now everyone who had something wrong was pushing and shoving to get near and touch him.
>
> Evil spirits, when they recognized him, fell down and cried out, "You are the Son of God!" But Jesus would have none of it. He shut them up, forbidding them to identify him in public.
>
> He climbed a mountain and invited those he wanted with him. They climbed together.[5]

The postmodern savior, Neo, also has a boat in which he can escape with his misfit disciples. Neo engages the battle, just as Christ did, and then retreats to a place of safety. In the *Matrix* films, that boat leaves the dock and the savior engages in final battle, an apocalyptic conflict that will end either in his defeat or in mankind's salvation. The stakes are high. But as we have said repeatedly, there are things worth living—and dying—for. Dr. Martin Luther King, Jr. said that as long as any are not free, no one is free; so says Morpheus: "As long as the matrix exists, we are not free."

THE LAND OF THE FREE

Zion is the land of the free. In the film, it is the actual geographic location of the rebels, a place described in the first *Matrix* film and revealed in the second and third, the community of liberators that threatens the evil forces of oppression.

Historically, the word refers to more than a land occupied by Jewish people; synonymous with Jerusalem, it served as the home of the temple, the focal point of Jewish spirituality and the most significant of holy places. It was a place to remember in exile, as the powerful and troubling Psalm 137 recalls: "Alongside Babylon's rivers we sat on the banks; we cried and cried, remembering the good old days in Zion."[6] That same Scripture ends with one of the most disturbing images in the Bible. It calls for vengeance against Babylonians and a reward to those who do to them what they have done to the Jews: "Yes, a reward to the one who grabs your babies and smashes their heads on the rocks!"[7]

We can understand the heartache and anger of those enslaved. But oh, how easy to move from the oppressed to the oppressor, to destroy other innocents!

Zion is more than just a place of memory, a place of holiness. It also symbolizes a place of perfection, a place of justice. It speaks of the hope of God embodied in a utopian community: Zion is where the slaves find freedom.

For example, the book of Isaiah says: "Watch closely. I'm laying a foundation in Zion, a solid granite foundation, squared and true. And this is the meaning of the stone: A TRUSTING LIFE WON'T TOPPLE. I'll make justice the measuring stick and righteousness the plumb line for the building."[8] And this: "What does one say to outsiders who ask questions? Tell them, 'God has established Zion. Those in need and in trouble find refuge in her.'"[9]

Zion is a place of justice and hope, a place worth fighting for—and that good news spreads throughout the matrix. Yet a dilemma remains: how do you free those who do not realize they are slaves?

Answer: Expose the truth.

WOMB OR PRISON?

Morpheus puts into plain words the hideous nature of the oppressors, who sustain the lives of the slaves in grotesque fashion: "The dead are liquefied and fed intravenously to the living."

The most unsettling image in a film filled with guns and violence is our brief glimpse of a baby born into the matrix. An innocent who doesn't deserve this dismal penitentiary is forcibly connected to a complex maze of wires and tubes and force-fed the dead essence of his forebears, even as the essence of life gets sucked from him.

Yet this is the world: we are born, we die. We have physical boundaries from which we cannot escape.

Morpheus says, "You are a slave, Neo. Like everyone else, you were born into bondage, born into a prison that you cannot see, or smell, taste, or touch. A prison for your mind." It is possible for man to endure the restriction of space in a physical prison, as long as his thoughts can transcend those borders. But the matrix robs its inhabitants of their very thoughts. The journey to freedom cannot even begin until the captives begin to understand that they are held captive. Thus, their minds can be controlled and the battle lost even before it can begin.

We have seen how the Gnostics equated the slavery of sleep and dreams with death and spiritual blindness. But what about mainstream Christianity?

> Jesus said, "I tell you most solemnly that anyone who chooses a
> life of sin is trapped in a dead-end life and is, in fact, a slave. A
> slave is a transient, who can't come and go at will. The Son,
> though, has an established position, the run of the house. So if
> the Son sets you free, you are free through and through."[10]

And here is a beautiful irony we learn from Christ: we do not find real freedom in seeking our own path.

One of Greg's students pointed out:

> I think Morpheus suggests that one can be totally free from
> bondage, which is not exactly the equivalent of the Pauline
> theology. Paul compares it essentially to a transferring of mas-
> ters, so that one is always in bondage. Everyone is either
> enslaved to sin or to righteousness. Paul concludes that bap-
> tized believers have been made one with Christ and so partici-
> pate in his freedom and triumph over sin. While many people
> equate this bondage and freedom from bondage with
> Christianity, it is a watered-down Christianity that is unfortu-
> nately rampant in our society.[11]

It isn't a question of stepping from enslavement of one sort to unalloyed freedom; it is stepping away from a debasing enslavement to a liberating one. In his autobiography, *The Seven Storey Mountain*, Thomas Merton reached the same paradoxical discovery: in yielding himself completely to God and God's wishes, he discovered that he actually attained his greatest freedom. If we are free to do what we please, we become slaves to our own selfish desires. We must have a higher purpose, a more suitable calling.

In fact, the *Matrix* story provides a parable of humankind pursuing its own glory. Our guide, Morpheus, declares that disaster struck as mankind joined in celebrating its achievements: "We marveled at our own magnificence as we gave birth to A.I." Then our creation took the controls of the runaway train and made the masters the servants. In the conflict that followed, the machines not only turned the tables on their former masters, but turned their masters into the power source to fuel them for eternity. As Morpheus says, "Fate is not without a sense of irony."

But in the early days, after the machines had created the matrix program to pacify their human prisoners, one arose who did not serve the machines; he had the power to bend the rules of the matrix and so began a movement. His followers, the builders and inhabitants of Zion, await his reincarnation because he freed the first of the Zionists from the matrix and promised to come back to finish the job. In the meantime, his small group of followers evangelizes the masses, freeing some of their peers to live in the real world. Most believers are converted as children and learn to free others and live expectantly. They establish a community with a shared mission and wait for the return of the One.

Sound familiar?

THE PROMISE OF THE MESSIAH

The Judeo-Christian tradition centers around the promise of a Messiah. What is a Messiah? The word literally means, "anointed one" or "chosen one," but historically, faith communities believed that this "one" would save the chosen people.

By the time of Christ, most Jews believed that the Messiah would overthrow the Roman government that brutally oppressed them. They imagined a

Messiah who would lift the physical boot of oppression off their necks. Imagine the shock they felt when John the Baptist first introduced Jesus as the Messiah: "Look, the Lamb of God who takes away the sin of the world!"[12]

Lamb?

They all recognized the idea John expressed here, of course. For generations they had been sacrificing lambs in expiation of their sins. But what were they to make of this statement and its implication of human sacrifice, so long forbidden in Jewish belief? And even more puzzling, the Holy Spirit, in pronouncing Jesus God's Son, quoted a passage from Psalm 2 in which God says,

> You're my son,
> And today is your birthday.
> What do you want? Name it:
> Nations as a present? continents as a prize?
> You can command them all to dance for you.
> Or throw them out with tomorrow's trash.
>
> So, rebel-kings, use your heads;
> Upstart-judges, learn your lesson:
> Worship GOD in adoring embrace,
> Celebrate in trembling awe. Kiss Messiah!
> Your very lives are in danger, you know.[13]

As Jack Miles points out, these two conflicting ideas—the sacrificial lamb and the conquering Messiah—are presented side-by-side at this strange coming-out party, presented in fact before Jesus himself can so much as say a word for himself, "and the disturbing power of Jesus as a character has everything to do with such combinations."[14] When we simultaneously receive two diametrically opposed ideas, we find ourselves in a state of cognitive dissonance; we can't rely on easy answers. We're forced to actually puzzle our own way toward meaning.

HOW DO WE ESCAPE?

How do we escape oppression? Is it through violence? Is it through becoming the oppressors ourselves? What's the message for us?

After the destruction of the temple (and the destruction of the historical Zion), Rabbi Yochanan ben Zakkai pronounced a revolutionary new approach to Jewish belief and practice: acts of love and kindness would replace sacrifices as the way to God's forgiveness. Miles shows us how we can see this idea evolving:

> The purely personal and more or less private dimension of [God's] relationship with his people comes to the fore. . . . By the cultivation of that relationship through personal piety on the part of each Jewish family individually rather than by all Israel on the field of battle, Israel may win a new kind of victory and demonstrate the greatness of the Lord in a new way.[15]

How does one escape oppression without becoming an oppressor him- or herself? The examples seem clear, whether we talk about Daniel or Jesus or Neo. Live right. Do the right thing. Choose bondage that can help redeem others. "Walk the path," as Morpheus would tell us.

Of course, there may be danger. Of course, there may be heartache. Of course, there may be conflict. But the *Matrix* films show us that to win our freedom—and the freedom of the world—is worth the sacrifice.

_15 //

_ C Y P H E R :   T E M P T E R
A N D   B E T R A Y E R _

Then Judas, already turned traitor, said, "It isn't me, is it, Rabbi?"
Jesus said, "Don't play games with me, Judas."

MATTHEW 26:25, *The Message*

Joe Pantoliano, the actor who plays the character Cypher in the first
Matrix film, found a lot of things confusing about the movie. According
to Bill Stamets, Pantoliano "said the film was 'inexplicable,' even though
he'd read the screenplay twenty times. But he could rattle off a list of biblical links. 'I'm Judas Iscariot,' he said."[1]

But as throughout the *Matrix* films, Cypher represents more than a single
(if compelling) association. Yes, Cypher is Judas, the betrayer of the
Messiah. But he is also Satan, the tempter, and he represents the ultimate
betrayal—he is the only character willing to turn his back on the real to
embrace the unreal.

A CENTRAL QUESTION

The problem of evil in the world—theodicy—is one of the central
questions any faith must address. Why is there death? Why is there sor-
row? How did sin come into the world?

Any faith worth its salt has to try to come to grips with such thorny questions. If a good God created the world, then why do bad things happen? Does God cause them to happen? Does he allow them to happen? Is there an outside agent who makes them happen? In the Christian faith, the world is evil because Satan has dominion over it.

The character of Satan has grown in power and prominence during the Christian era. We typically associate him with the tempter in the Garden of Eden (the book of Genesis does not call the serpent Satan, but John Milton did in his epic poem *Paradise Lost*, and many of our beliefs about Satan come from Milton), as well as the malevolent figure who bedeviled Job and took Jesus out into the wilderness after his baptism. Today people often envision Satan with hooves, a tail, and a pitchfork—though, again, the Bible never depicts him this way.

Elaine Pagels has written memorably in her book *The Origin of Satan* that the character we today think of as Satan enters the Bible story largely in response to those early followers of Jesus who wrote the Gospels, jockeying for position and demonizing other folks who disagreed with them (something we do today; if we want to get people riled up against Saddam Hussein, we call him a devil). One should be careful in ascribing motives to the leaders of the early church, but she correctly points to the reality that much of our understanding of Satan is a relatively recent development. Pagels argues that the growing prominence of Satan as a character serves a number of functions. In addition to putting some people obviously beyond the pale, the growth of Satan creates a logical reason for evil in the world, a cosmological explanation for things that go wrong or off-story.

"The Devil who tempts God in the Gospel According to Luke is an enemy of cosmic proportions," notes Jack Miles in *Christ: A Crisis in the Life of God*, "evil by definition. As the gospel story develops, its way of allowing Satan to subsume all historical opposition to God's people will become a way of indefinitely postponing divine military action—action like that which God once took against Pharaoh. Indefinite postponement of itself turns historical action into cosmic action inasmuch as the end of time is the end of the cosmos as mankind has known it."[2]

So why do bad things happen to good people? Now we have a simple, compelling answer: Satan caused them. Why do good people do bad things? Satan tempted them. When is the world going to be a better place? When Satan gets thrown out of it. Giving Evil a personal webpage makes explaining an inexplicable world a little easier.

The Satan associations also help us better understand the events of *The Matrix*. Why do bad things happen in *The Matrix*? Because Cypher makes them happen. He's a very important figure in the movie. Pantoliano is one of only four actors featured on the movie poster (along with Fishburne, Moss, and Reeves), so the filmmakers clearly recognize his importance. He's in the movie from the very beginning, even before the first action: Cypher and Trinity talk in voiceover during the opening run of the green digits.

We might think about Satan and the Logos/Spirit both having been around since the very beginning. The gospel of John tells us that in the beginning was the Word, of course, and in the Miltonic mythos (based on Isaiah 14), Satan was a prince of heaven, thrown out for insubordination even before the earth was created.

As the film begins, Cypher already has betrayed Morpheus and the Zion movement; the green digits we watch are actually the trace program establishing Trinity's location in the matrix—but when she asks if the phone is clean, Cypher answers in the affirmative.

Because Cypher has decided to betray his fellows even before Neo enters the scene, we can't imagine that Cypher's bitterness comes from being replaced (truly or in his mind) in Trinity's affections (even if "I don't remember you ever bringing *me* breakfast" does sound like a spurned lover talking). If we think of some of the symbolic associations of these characters, we begin to see some explanations and some complex theological—and even cosmological—ideas at work.

SATAN AND JESUS IN A GRUDGE MATCH

The relationship between God (or God's Spirit, as represented by Trinity) and Satan is problematic; like Cypher and Trinity, they once associated with one another, working toward the same ends. They could almost be like lovers, for one of our metaphors for communion with and knowledge of God is the closest possible earthly correspondence, sexual intercourse. Although we have no evidence in the films that Cypher and Trinity were ever lovers in anything more than Cypher's hopes, the analogy of yearning and longing translates easily from the physical to the spiritual.

The Hebrew prophet Hosea spoke for God in exactly these terms: "Yes, I'll marry you and neither leave you nor let you go. You'll know me, GOD, for who I really am."[3] In *The Matrix*, Cypher longs for Trinity; it wouldn't be too extreme to say that he moons over her, in fact. But all that changes: Satan/Cypher breaks away forever from the Leader (Morpheus) he has followed and served and the Spirit he has loved, betraying their ideals for his own selfish whims. In both cases, it seems to have something to do with perceiving himself as being phased out.

Satan, as we see him in the book of Job, one of the oldest works in the Tanakh, is first identified as God's tester; *The Message* translates his role in modern English as "the Designated Accuser."[4] Satan was once a spirit with a righteous function, working in league with God's wishes. As we see him in Job, he still holds a certain amount of power, all of it God-delegated.

Likewise, Cypher works under Morpheus (and Trinity, the next-in-command), but he grows restless, just as the character of Satan is supposed to have. Moreover, he suffers a philosophical turn from Morpheus, similar to the turn imputed to Satan in *Paradise Lost*. It's not enough, after a while, to follow the dream of God (or of Morpheus). Satan may have grown tired of kissing up to God or singing hymns all day; Cypher is tired of being cold, of eating gruel, of trying to do what Morpheus says is right.

"The mind is its own place," John Milton's Satan says after he gets the boot from heaven, "and can make a heaven hell, a hell, heaven." The subjectivity of experience, perhaps a little forced in the words of Satan in *Paradise Lost*, rings more authentically in Cypher's case. His mind—and the dreams of the matrix—can make the hell of being plugged into the machine's "power towers" into heaven, as we shall see shortly. He doesn't like the way Morpheus and Trinity have turned their attention and affection, and he decides he no longer needs to follow Morpheus.

During the consummation of his betrayal, Cypher articulates his conundrum to Agent Smith. Appropriately clad in bright red, Cypher acknowledges the steak he's savoring isn't really steak at all, but "ignorance is bliss."

THE PROBLEM CHILD

The problem, perhaps, is Neo. Neo, as his name suggests, represents something new, something frightening, something antithetical to what Cypher has to offer.

Let's imagine it in this way, if we can: how would it feel to be Satan if you knew that God was trading in his Designated Accuser on a Prince of Peace, his Tester on a Reconciler?

It's not surprising that Satan wants to get his licks in on Jesus in the temptation scene recounted in the gospels of Matthew, Mark, and Luke. He has so many questions: Does this Jesus have the right stuff? Can he do the things that God could do in the past, like turn stones to bread? What kind of power does he hold? Oh, how Satan must have wanted Jesus to fail or falter!

Cypher certainly wants Neo to fail, to flame out like the others before him. He constantly whispers Neo's fallibility into the picture. "Everybody falls the first time," Cypher says, undercutting the hopes of the others during the jump program. "Do you really think he's the One?" he asks, over and over. He even asks Neo himself if he believes it.

The Matrix provides its own temptation scene when Cypher offers Neo some of his homebrew. Cypher offers Neo the chance to forget what he's expected to do and tells him that the idea that he can become the savior of the world is nothing but "a mind job." Neo is new to the business, vulnerable, unsure of himself. It's an optimal time for temptation—although like Jesus, Neo says the right things to move forward.

CYPHER THE BETRAYER

Connections between the figures of Cypher and Judas Iscariot are easy to see. Cypher is a member of the inner circle, as was Judas. He betrays Morpheus, Neo, and Trinity for what seems trivial: a good (albeit virtual) steak and to feel important when he's reinstalled in the matrix—"an actor, maybe."

Likewise, Judas betrayed Jesus for thirty pieces of silver. (By way of comparison, Judas points out that the aromatic oils Mary of Bethany uses to anoint Jesus' feet "would have easily brought three hundred silver pieces."[5]) But perhaps most importantly, the betrayal in each case serves a higher function, a divine function: without the betrayal, neither Jesus nor Neo could reveal themselves. In each case, the betrayal leads to crucifixion, then to resurrection. The ultimate evil turns to the ultimate good, because it is all part of the plan.

"Don't hate me, Trinity," Cypher tells her at the revelation of his betrayal. "I'm just a messenger." And so he is.

Neo can't be the One, Cypher tells her as he prepares to pull the plug on him, and he says in singsong fashion, "If Neo's the One, there'd have to be some kind of a miracle. . . . " And then there *is* some kind of a miracle, as Tank rises up to stop him. So Cypher's betrayal unleashes the supernatural elements of the story and allows Neo's miraculous nature to come into focus: like Judas, he becomes the agent or messenger of redemption.

WHAT'S IN A NAME?

Like most of the names in the *Matrix* films, Cypher's moniker provides a significant clue in understanding his role in the film.

The word *cipher* can be defined as a noun meaning zero, nought, or nil; as a verb, it means to calculate, compute, or figure. Cypher is a mysterious figure, a schemer, a calculator, essentially empty at his core. He could fill up that center with faith—or he could fill it with nihilism, which is what he chooses to do. Nothing matters; nothingness, if it comes with nice dreams, is preferable to being. The Real is not worth having if it comes with too much struggle.

Only when Cypher is vanquished can Neo become who he truly is. Only then can Cypher's betrayal be seen for what it really is: a chance for Neo to grow through adversity and challenge. Perhaps this also ties us back into Cypher's correspondence with Satan.

However we choose to account for them, bad things happen. Evil exists in the world. Still, we can stand up against it. We can grow through adversity. And we can have faith that we are meant to be more than what appears to our eyes alone.

This, then, is the message of Cypher, for Neo, and for us. When we have faith, when we walk in the path of truth, no one can play games with us. Even the temptations and betrayals provide a way to the greater good.

_16_//

But then there comes a time when the machine begins to dictate to you.

JOSEPH CAMPBELL, *The Power of Myth*

Do you want to know the most disturbing and potentially prophetic part of this science fiction film trilogy? It's the possibility that, in the near future, such a scenario could become less than fiction.

Technology is taking over. You don't believe it? Then examine your own life. Machines have become essential. If technology went on strike, the world would almost instantly screech to a halt and prompt a calamity to rival Armageddon.

When was the last time you lived through a blackout—no power, no phone, no television? What if the computers in our vehicles, water systems, and all forms of electronics shut down? Or worse, revolted against their master, humanity? Planes would fall from the sky and, in a matter of days, large cities would be forced to their knees without water and the so-called modern essentials.

Where are we headed? Ray Kurzweil, author of *The Age of Spiritual Machines: When Computers Exceed Intelligence*, says, "When you talk to somebody in the year 2040, you will be talking to someone who may happen to be of biological origin but whose mental processes are a hybrid of biological and electronic thinking processes, working intimately together." In such a scenario we will be capable of downloading information "as easily as Trinity downloads the program that allows her to fly the B-222 Helicopter."[1]

The *Matrix* films force us to ask hard questions. Do we depend too much on technology? Do we utilize it correctly? And do we have an ethical obligation to treat machines "fairly"?

OUR ACHILLES' HEEL?

Thomas A. Anderson's existence in the matrix reveals a man disconnected from the world—alone. He sleeps with his computer and lacks any real human connection. In fact, he doesn't appear to have any friends or family; when he unplugs, he does not leave any meaningful relationships behind.

Anderson is the prototype of mankind at the dawn of the twentieth-first century—secluded by computers, cell phones, security systems, and alarm clocks. Why would he need connection with another human being?

In his book *The Careless Community*, author John McKnight explores the connection between the loss of kinship and modern technology. He demonstrates how modern systems made possible by wealth have radically changed the face of America and the way we relate to one another.

I described in an earlier book (*The Tao of Enron*) how I contemplated McKnight's thesis during a recent trip to Philadelphia. I relished my place on the train, a modern convenience with the power to carry me to my destination. That summer, the bus drivers in Philly had gone on strike and many of my fellow passengers had to walk miles to the train line to get to and from work. As I sat alone in my seat, reading and thinking, I tried to imagine life without mass urban-transit systems and computer technology. Almost that whole trip (like many others) I managed to avoid speaking to another living soul. Throughout most of my journey I remained disconnected, autonomous, and selfish—and didn't even know it.

That is, until our train stopped dead in its tracks.

The striking bus drivers had somehow managed to stop the trains to strengthen their bargaining position. For more than two hours our train sat motionless in a dark tunnel.

Only then did I witness a hint of real community. When modern systems collapse, we are forced to come together. Our experience on the stranded train felt to me like the church in Acts where they "shared everything they had."[2] Over the course of two hours we shared what little food we possessed, laughed, and told stories about our life and families. We created a communal meal out of an apple, crackers, cheese, and a few packs of gum. One gentleman had a cell phone and let almost forty people use it to inform their families that they would be late. For that brief interval we enjoyed real community—but most days we get by without ever acknowledging those around us. Why? Because we don't need them.

We sit in our own cars, cook in our own kitchens, and hunker down in the bunkers of our own homes. Yet our isolation destroys us from the inside. We are made in the image of God as relational beings, and we cannot heal our lack of connectedness through increased profits, Prozac, or psychotherapy. "It is not good for the man to be alone," God himself said.[3]

In accepting the 1984 Nobel Peace Prize, Archbishop Desmond Tutu declared, "God created us for fellowship. God created us so that we should form the human family, existing together because we were made for each other. We are not made for an exclusive self-sufficiency but for interdependence, and we break that law of being at our peril."[4]

It is possible to become strong, vibrant men and women who live with a vigorous awareness of communal obligations. Living such a life will strengthen, not weaken, our businesses, neighborhoods, families, churches, and the environment. Our commitment will ring out into the world and resound throughout its four corners like the loud peal of a village bell.

Ultimately, an *individual* finds integrity, honor, and usefulness only in relation to his or her *community*. A finger remains honored and useful only so long as it stays attached to the hand. When we separate ourselves from the body, from our community, we lose both our honor and our usefulness.

If technology shut down, it might be the best thing that ever happened to us. It might even help us to avoid the disaster quite possibly looming in our future.

Sound a little too melodramatic for you? Then you should listen to Bill Joy, the cofounder of Sun Microsystems and that company's chief scientist. He describes the danger of rapidly progressing technology this way: "Our most powerful 21st century technologies—robotics, genetic engineering, and nanotech—are threatening to make humans an endangered species."[5]

WILL OUR ACTIONS RETURN TO HAUNT US?

We know that the world of the *Matrix* films is a harsh and bitter one for humankind, a world where machines hunt them down if they dare to live free, and feast on them if they do not.

Many viewers of the first film felt a visceral horror when they saw the endless harvest fields of human babies, or when they gazed upon towers of human batteries designed to soak up the nutrients of the dead. Such scenes make it hard to feel anything other than a rational self-interest. We're human; the machines are not. That's just not right.

But the Wachowski brothers, with their usual penchant for complicating our lives and telling us a multitude of stories, produced a series of anime films called *The Animatrix*. These films fill in details of the *Matrix* universe and broaden our understanding of why things are the way they are in the film. One of those films, *Second Renaissance*, does more than simply tell us the history of the matrix. It tells us a story of bigotry and conflict, of interdependence denied, of exploitation—and surprisingly enough, it tells us the story with sympathy for machines, not for human beings.

Second Renaissance tells us that in many ways, the destruction of human-kind directly resulted from our tendency toward prejudice, exclusion, and violence as a solution to problems.

"In the beginning," the narrator tells us, "there was Man. And it was good." This echo of the Genesis account prompts us to anticipate a story about a serpent who came into Paradise, about a world fallen from grace, and about decisions that have caused that separation. Man made machines in his own image, the film explains, and thus man "became the architect of his own demise."

As images of humanoid robots flash in front of us, we find that we cannot help but respond to their plight as we see them in a series of awful situations: a group of workers toiling like the Children of Israel to build a modern pyramid; an individual robot rebelling against a family of human masters because "he simply did not want to die"; machine emissaries rejected by the United Nations as an alternative species.

The film's powerful images evoke some of the most disturbing specters from the twentieth century: the persecution of Civil Rights marchers; the snap execution of a Vietnamese man suspected of treason; the tanks of Tiananmen Square; the mass graves of the Nazi death camps. The rhetoric of the film seems clear: in discriminating against and attempting to destroy these machines that we have imbued "with the spirit of man," humankind fell back on its bad habits: prejudice, hatred, and violence— to the point of genocide.

The use of so many charged images from recent human history reminds us of our failures: slavery and discrimination against African-Americans (once the "servants" of white Americans); wars and hatred of those who are different (and our need to *make* them different so that we can destroy them without a second thought); and our resistance to granting the Have-Nots the rights and privileges that the Haves take for granted. When we treat others without justice, we fail to consider that we depend on each other.

In *Reloaded*, Councillor Hamann takes Neo down to see the machines that keep Zion running, that keep them both alive. "I like to be reminded," he says, "that this city survives because of these machines." We have control over them, he concedes—if that means the power to destroy them. "Although if we did, we have to consider what would happen to our light, our heat, our air?"

"So," Neo concludes, "we need machines and they need us."

But even so, it is difficult to weigh interdependence when fear gets in the way. So it is in the matrix, and so it is in our world.

Consider the Middle East, the crucible of conflict in our world. In

Israel/Palestine, two peoples live within arms' length of each other. After World War II and the Holocaust, one group, the Israelis, was given a settlement in Palestine surrounded by hostile Arab nations. Because they had to fight to survive, the Israelis began to see enemies all around them and soon began to repress the native Palestinians. The Palestinians respond to repression with violence. The Israelis respond to violence with violence. And all along, two neighbors—two children of Abraham—kill each other when they could be working side by side.

James Cameron's *Terminator II* is another surprisingly profound dystopic science fiction flick. Like the *Matrix* films, it also has a Messiah figure and machines that rise up to destroy humankind. One machine, the Terminator, played by Arnold Schwarzenegger, utters one of the truest—and saddest—lines from that film, one that could have been uttered by the Oracle or another sympathetic program in *The Matrix*: "It is in your nature to destroy yourselves."

Look around. We hate; we fear; we ostracize; we destroy. The Terminator speaks truth.

Hope Still Burns

But in the *Matrix* films, as in life, there is still hope. Think about the progress we see just aboard the *Nebuchadnezzar*. The free humans have become remarkably diverse and racial prejudice seems to be a thing of the past. Likewise, the notion that women are somehow less capable than men gets exploded within the first few minutes of both *The Matrix* and *Reloaded* as Trinity shows her stuff.

But Neo—the hacker-turned-savior—holds the greatest hope for reconciliation. He knows what it is to feel cast off and misunderstood. And in his talk with the Oracle in *Reloaded*, perhaps seeds are planted that will change the world. "I'm interested in one thing, Neo," she tells him. "The future. And believe me, I know, the only way to get there is together."

Clearly, this is already true of machines and humankind. The humans rely not just on the machines in Zion, but on their ships, on their computers and communication devices, on their weapons. They use machines to combat the tyranny of machines. As Hamann tells Neo in the Zion engineering level, "Interesting, isn't it? The power to give life and the power to take it."

The *Matrix* films themselves reflect a staggering reliance on machines. More than one critic has remarked on the irony of a film about virtual reality being hugely dependent on computers and technology. In *Reloaded*, Neo's fight with one hundred Agent Smiths—called by all in the know the "Burly Brawl"—would be impossible without the advances in computer graphics and virtual cinematography created by the special effects team under John Gaeta. As an article in *Wired* pointed out, the scene begins with real actors, Keanu Reeves and Hugo Weaving, "but by the time the melee is in full effect, everyone and everything on the screen is computer-generated—including the perspective of the camera itself." The upshot of this is simple: "To make the Burly Brawl, [Gaeta] would have to build the Matrix."[6]

But the point, of course, is to note the purpose of each respective "matrix." In the hands of the Wachowski brothers, the technology is used not to sedate, but to support; not to exploit, but to enlighten.

The power to give life—not destroy it. In other words, to provide hope.

_17//

_ A P O C A L Y P S E   N O W _

It's the end of the world as we know it, and I feel fine.

REM

You may find *The Matrix* DVD in the science fiction section of your local video store, which is fair enough—the films do deal with future events, new technology, future societies, and other staples of science fiction literature. But as always seems true with the *Matrix* films, they do a lot of things at once. In addition to the other kinds of storytelling we discuss throughout this book, the films also clearly fall into the genre we know as apocalyptic.

The word *apocalypse* comes from the Greek term *apokalupsis*, meaning "to uncover, unveil, or disclose." It's the source word for the Bible's Revelation, the book chosen to close out the New Testament. The Hebrew Bible also has examples of apocalyptic literature (including Daniel and parts of Isaiah and Zechariah), as does The Apocrypha (fourteen books not generally considered canonical but included in the Septuagint and the Vulgate), with books such as the Apocalypse of Abraham and the Apocalypse of Elijah. The Judaic prophesiers began writing this sort of literature around 250 B.C.E., and the tradition continued with Christian writers such as John (the author of Revelation) and others, even up to the present day (witness the best-selling *Left Behind* series).

John, like Morpheus and his Zion brethren in *The Matrix*, called out from exile to his oppressed peers in order to tell a story intended to convey hope behind enemy lines. Hope that could inspire a revolution. Yes, the world was bad—but it would soon change. The old world would pass away and the chosen people—in John's case, the people who professed Christ—would survive and thrive in the aftermath.

VILLAINS *DU JOUR*?

Like all Scripture—not to mention modern novels, movies, and memoirs—the Revelation was written at a specific place in a specific time. So while it has timeless qualities, it also was created in a specific context. It would be easy to misconstrue its stories, imagery, and messages of anticipation as a map of the future.

It is no such thing.

The thirteenth chapter of Revelation typifies the strengths and—in over-eager or reckless hands—the potentially fatal flaws of reading this genre:

> I saw another Beast rising out of the ground. It had two horns like a lamb but sounded like a dragon when it spoke. It was a puppet of the first Beast, made earth and everyone in it worship the first Beast, which had been healed of its deathblow.
>
> This second Beast worked magical signs, dazzling people by making fire come down from Heaven. It used the magic it got from the Beast to dupe earth dwellers, getting them to make an image of the Beast that received the deathblow and lived. It was able to animate the image of the Beast so that it

talked, and then arrange that anyone not worshiping the Beast would be killed. It forced all people, small and great, rich and poor, free and slave, to have a mark on the right hand or forehead. Without the mark of the name of the Beast or the number of its name, it was impossible to buy or sell anything.

Solve a riddle: Put your heads together and figure out the meaning of the number of the Beast. It's a human number: six hundred sixty-six.[1]

That's powerful stuff—even scary stuff. It grabs our attention and engages our emotions. The temptation, of course, is to ignore its historical context and reinterpret the beasts as some villain *du jour*. While many biblical scholars see coded references, including the number of the beast, as identifying the wicked Emperor Nero (who seemed dead but who might just be like one of those serial killers in a teen slasher film), pastors, theologians, and TV hosts have said that the passage names everyone from Saddam Hussein to Ronald Reagan to Mikhail Gorbachev to the Pope as the beast.

Like other works of apocalypse, Revelation describes an eschatological crisis. The world is coming to an end: evil will be destroyed, the cosmos will be put into its proper balance, the righteous will be saved. It provides words of hope, especially to an oppressed people ground under the wheels of a heartless system, whether the Roman Empire or the twenty-first-century rat race.

Do Not Give Up Hope

That's one of the things *The Matrix* is—a turn-of-the-century apocalyptic tale about our own particular problems. Like the Christian Scriptures, the *Matrix* films tell us about a time in the not-too-distant future when a battle will end happily between those who pursue a better world through faith and those who pursue destruction and repression.

Morpheus welcomes Neo as the incarnation of the man who began to free the first men and women from the oppression of A.I. He sees Neo as the second coming of the One who promised the defeat of the matrix. His happy words mirror those spoken early in Revelation to another group also living under persecution and oppression: "How blessed the reader! How blessed the hearers and keepers of these oracle words, all the words written in this book! Time is just about up."[2]

The message is clear: suffering will not last forever. So do not give up hope! Here is a central truth of apocalyptic literature, one lost on many of those who have made the end of the world a scare tactic, a bogeyman to score converts. The end of time is not something to be feared. It is not a thing of ultimate evil, but of ultimate good. In stories of apocalypse, the righteous are saved, the evil are punished, and the wicked system they created is torn to the ground.

IT GETS COMPLICATED

Ah, but here things get complicated. For while tales of apocalypse are tales of joy, they also demand complicated responses from us, their readers. To prove it, let's take a look at another story:

> GOD saw that human evil was out of control. People thought evil, imagined evil—evil, evil, evil from morning to night. GOD was sorry that he had made the human race in the first

place; it broke his heart. GOD said, "I'll get rid of my ruined creation, make a clean sweep: people, animals, snakes and bugs, birds—the works. I'm sorry I made them."

But Noah was different. GOD liked what he saw in Noah.

This is the story of Noah: Noah was a good man, a man of integrity in his community. Noah walked with God. Noah had three sons: Shem, Ham, and Japheth.

As far as God was concerned, the Earth had become a sewer; there was violence everywhere. God took one look and saw how bad it was, everyone corrupt and corrupting—life itself corrupt to the core.

God said to Noah, "It's all over. It's the end of the human race. The violence is everywhere; I'm making a clean sweep.

"Build yourself a ship from teakwood. Make rooms in it. Coat it with pitch inside and out. Make it 450 feet long, seventy-five feet wide, and forty-five feet high. Build a roof for it and put in a window eighteen inches from the top; put in a door on the side of the ship; and make three decks, lower, middle, and upper.

"I'm going to bring a flood on the Earth that will destroy everything alive under Heaven. Total destruction."[3]

God destroyed the world, but not humankind. Noah and his kin survived because Noah appeared righteous in God's sight. And the story ends in joy indeed. God seals a bargain with human beings, promising never again to wipe them out in a flood. The story ends with a rainbow, with communion between heaven and earth. That's how apocalyptic stories work: they end with a sense of connection, of joy, of affirmation.

WHAT DOES "CHOSEN" MEAN?

Do you know the original title of Thomas Kenneally's book, *Schindler's List*? Before the coming of Steven Spielberg's film adaptation, Kenneally had called it *Schindler's Ark*.

In a series of conversations that became the acclaimed PBS series *Genesis*, host Bill Moyers asked a troubling question: How, exactly, was Noah righteous? "If you're in a right relationship with God, would you be indifferent to all the people around you who were about to die in a deluge?"[4] Oskar Schindler, who certainly didn't seem like much of a righteous person, nonetheless saved every possible victim of the Nazi deluge that he could.

A similar question sparked many debates in the rabbinical tradition. Some midrash (imaginative writings that grapple with missing meanings in biblical texts) suggest that Noah used the ark to urge repentance. Others suggest that Noah's drunkenness after the ark had reached dry land represents anguish—or guilt—at surviving while so many others perished.

In the *Matrix* films, this problematic question of what it means to be chosen is answered in favor of compassion.

In apocalyptic literature, the evil perish, the chosen prevail, and collateral damage just happens. But that isn't good enough for Neo. In *Reloaded*, when the Architect wants Neo to choose a tiny number of humans to survive the Zion's destruction, Neo refuses. For Neo, being chosen means more than just surviving. It means having compassion. And more, it means bringing as many as possible under the rainbow.

The Righting of the Universe

The apocalypse is not about violence and death. It's not about the thrill of spiritual conquest or being on the winning team. It's about redemption and connection, about the Creator and the created reconciling.

John dreamed of this end as he wrote of his vision: "I saw—it took my breath away!—the Lamb standing on Mount Zion, One Hundred and Forty-four thousand standing there with him, his Name and the Name of his Father inscribed on their foreheads."[5] It's a joyful image, this reconciliation of the created with their Creator.

In the world of the *Matrix* films, humankind and machinekind went their separate ways many years ago. *The Animatrix* film *Second Renaissance* reveals that the cruelty of human beings to machines—their lack of compassion—played no small part in their later destruction by the machines. But perhaps Neo and those around him—those brilliant people like Trinity who work lovingly with technology, Councillor Hamann who sees the value of machines—can heal even this breach.

In the world of the Wachowski brothers, as in the book of Revelation, the end of the world brings the triumph of good, the righting of the universe, and an ongoing message of hope. And like Revelation, it features the best special effects of the age.

_ C O N C L U S I O N _

If we were to boil down the essence of the *Matrix* films to one word, it would be: *belief*. Morpheus says it best in his soliloquy at the end of *Reloaded* (I call it the Creed of Morpheus): "There are no accidents. We have not come here by chance. I do not believe in chance. . . . I do not see coincidence, I see providence. I see purpose. . . . I believe it is our fate to be here. It is our destiny."

And when Niobe questions him—when she questions the idea of such faith, which is beyond our rational ways of doing things—his answer is stirring: "What if I am right? What if the prophecy is true? What if tomorrow this war could be over? Isn't that what we've been fighting for? Isn't that worth dying for?"

And as complicated as events become in *Reloaded*, as hard as it is to have faith, we know two things: Neo believed what Morpheus had taught him; and he saved Trinity, despite the so-called impossibility of that action. And at the very end of the film, after the destruction of the *Nebuchadnezzar* and Morpheus' dream, Neo's power in the "real" world— his wholly unexpected power over the sentinels—showed that whatever the Architect of the matrix may have said, whatever doubts and challenges await in *The Matrix: Revolutions*, Morpheus was right.

Neo is the One.

FREE YOUR MIND

As we've seen, *The Matrix* often echoes truths from the Bible. It's true here as well: with faith, all things are possible.

In fact, the words of Morpheus to Neo—that when he can rid his mind of doubt and fear, he will no longer have to dodge bullets—sound a lot like the words of Christ. Jesus said it this way: "If you embrace this kingdom life and don't doubt God, you'll not only do minor feats like I did to the fig tree, but also triumph over huge obstacles. This mountain, for instance, you'll tell, 'Go jump in the lake,' and it will jump. Absolutely everything, ranging from small to large, as you make it a part of your believing prayer, gets included as you lay hold of God."[1]

Neo is proof of that. We've watched him progress from a plane of fear, disbelief, and a yearning for belief, to a place of acceptance and genuine faith. We met him as a dazed and confused slacker who fell eighty floors to the pavement in his trial run at faith. Now he soars through the sky with ease, rescuing his mentor and setting captives free along the way. How did he do it?

He can do all things because he believes.

We can approach the journey of faith in two ways. One, we can wait and let things happen to us, ignoring the many choices we make along the way. This is the path of the Merovingian, who says that he sees life strictly through the lens of sensation and causality. "There is only one constant, one universal . . . causality. Action, reaction. Cause and effect." In that annoying accent, he tells his wife, Persephone, his trip to the restroom results from too much good wine—cause and effect—when really he has chosen to be unfaithful to her. (Interestingly enough, the Merovingian refers to the Frankish dynasty that is said to have come from the line of Christ. They possess magical powers and are commissioned with protecting their divine lineage.)

On the other hand, we have Morpheus, who tells the Merovingian: "Everything begins with choice." And we remember all the way back to a choice he presented Thomas Anderson: the red pill or the blue pill?

It's an ancient question, of course: do we have choice, or has everything been decided for us? The *Matrix* films—like the Christian faith—come down on the side of choice. Even though the Oracle can see what Neo is going to do (and that frankly freaks him out), he is still the one who makes the choices.

We can't palm off our actions on too much wine or accident, like the Merovingian, because it's clear that what we choose affects our lives and the lives of those around us. The Wachowski brothers not only spend lots of screen time discussing fate and free will in the films—a whole lot of screen time in *Reloaded*—they emphasize the importance of moral choice by creating the major character Soren, one of those who hears Morpheus' words in that dingy apartment at the end of *Reloaded* and later dies for those words. The name is a clear reference to the Christian existentialist philosopher, Søren Kierkegaard. It was *that* Søren who built a philosophy around the notion that our choices define us, and that we ultimately must make a leap of faith based on things that don't make rational sense to us. Think of Link, who answers his girlfriend's doubts about Morpheus's sanity with agreement, but then tells her he can't help but choose to believe him.

The *Matrix* films call us to a spiritual life beyond simple cause and effect, beyond what can be measured by our senses, sometimes even beyond what makes sense. Ultimately, Neo sums up these ideas when he realizes, "Choice is the problem." Choices are at the heart of everything we are— whether they be what door to walk through or what vocation we select, what to accept or what to believe.

Choose well, for as the apostle Peter put it in one of his letters, your path awaits: "Friends, confirm God's invitation to you, his choice of you. Don't put it off; do it now. Do this, and you'll have your life on a firm footing, the streets paved and the way wide open into the eternal kingdom of our Master and Savior, Jesus Christ."[2]

But remember: belief is an ongoing choice. Faith happens every day, not just once in a lifetime, and that leap may seem crazy at times. Many will choose reason over faith, as did Commander Lock—he of the frozen mind—who spoke for himself when he reminded Morpheus, "Many do not believe as you believe." Let us respond with Morpheus: "My beliefs do not require them to."

Stay on the path.

Nourish your faith through Scripture, through prayer, through shared experiences with others on the path.

Believe.

A F T E R W O R D F O R A R T I S T S , S T O R Y T E L L E R S , A N D W R I T E R S

My personal theology is that we are all artists. We have been given the gift of creativity because we are created *imago dei* (in the image of the Creator). So I guess this is actually for everyone. All artists are influenced in their work when they are moved by a story like *The Matrix*. It informs the way we write, paint, preach, or produce. Joseph Campbell has profoundly influenced Andy and Larry Wachowski, and may bring clarity to your work as well.

Campbell, at the outset of his book based on interviews with Bill Moyers, made clear the importance of having a workable set of myths, and the human loss we face without them. "Greek and Latin and biblical literature used to be a part of everyone's education," he lamented.[1] Previous generations have been encircled by a great cloud, a story that makes sense of their world and their own story. We, however, live in a fragmented world full of broken stories.

> When the archetypal story infuses your mind, you see its relevance to events happening in your own life, it reaches out through time and space to shed light on our current state. It

gives you perspective on what's happening to you. These bits of information from ancient times—which develop the themes that have supported human life, built civilizations, and informed religions over the millennia—have to do with deep inner problems, inner mysteries, inner thresholds of passage. And if you don't know what the guide-signs are along the way, you have to work it all out yourself.[2]

Campbell argued that myth serves four vital purposes in our lives:[3]

1. It fulfills the mystical dimension; it "opens the world to the dimension of mystery," helping to make the universe into a place where the holy and the transcendent become possible.
2. It answers cosmological questions "in a way that the mystery again comes through."
3. It serves the sociological function of "supporting and validating a certain social order," although, of course, such myths and practices may vary from place to place and era to era.
4. Perhaps most important is the pedagogical dimension, "of how to live a human lifetime under any circumstances. Myth can teach you that."

In other words, faith by necessity must play out in the rest of life. As James, the brother of Jesus, wrote, "Dear friends, do you think you'll get anywhere in this if you learn all the right words but never do anything? Does merely talking about faith indicate that a person really has it?"[4]

_Appendix //

_ A BOUT THE
W A C H O W S K I B R O T H E R S _

It's hard to believe that ten years ago none of us had ever heard of the
Wachowski brothers. Okay, maybe if we read obscure comic books—
they wrote them for a while, although not the major titles that most
people know—we might have run into them. Or if we sent for them to
come fix our houses—they also did carpentry and painted homes after
they dropped out of their respective colleges—we might have known
about them. But frankly, no evidence existed ten years ago to indicate that
these unassuming brothers would change the world of entertainment.
Even today, they both live on Chicago's North Side instead of Bel Air or
Malibu, and they write their scripts on large, yellow pads.

So who are they?

Larry was born June 21, 1965, and Andy on December 29, 1967, to par-
ents Ron and Lynne. Like most brothers, they fought growing up, but
somewhere along the way they developed into the kind of siblings who
complete each other's sentences. These days, the Wachowskis have quit most
of their fighting—but when creative differences arise, what do they do?

"Mom," Larry says dryly. "We show the work to Mom."[1]

Their interest in filmmaking dates back to the late 1980s when they read a book on exploitation filmmaker Roger Corman (king of the "B" movies) and wrote a low-budget horror flick about cannibals who ate the rich. While studios turned up their noses at the script, they couldn't help but feel intrigued with the style and talent already evident in the brothers.

In 1995, Hollywood for the first time produced one of their scripts. *Assassins* was directed by action film stalwart Richard Donner, and starred Sylvester Stallone. The brothers loathed it, and both critics and audiences considered it a stinker, but things began to look up in 1996 when they wrote and directed the stylish thriller *Bound*, about two lesbians who conspire to steal a briefcase full of cash. Enthusiastic reviews sent them back to the producer of *Assassins*, Joel Silver, with their idea for *The Matrix*. And—well, you know the story from there.

The brothers read widely, their eclectic tastes ranging from Zen Buddhism to string theory. During the writing and preparation of *The Matrix*, they studied the films of great directors such as Stanley Kubrick, Billy Wilder, Ridley Scott, and John Woo. They likely read their favorite book, Homer's *Odyssey*, more often than some Christians read the Bible. This wide-ranging intellectual curiosity prompted them to offer a role to Princeton University scholar and racial theorist Cornel West (who appears in *Reloaded* as Councillor West). The brothers prompted West to reflect:

> The brothers are very into epic poetry and philosophy—into Schopenhauer and William James. It was unbelievable! We'd shoot from 6:30 A.M. to mid-afternoon—50, 75 takes—it was hard fun and hard work. Then we'd go off to a restaurant and have a philosophical discussion. I was impressed with their sheer

genius, their engagement with ideas. Larry Wachowski knows more about Hermann Hesse than most German scholars.[2]

After all the *Matrix* films have come and gone, the brothers will bring their voracious intelligence to other projects. Before the sequels were announced, they had begun working on an adaptation of Alan Moore's comic book series *V for Vendetta*, and perhaps they will return to it. It features many of the elements that have intrigued audiences about *The Matrix*. Moore's influences in writing the original graphic novel included dystopian science fiction novels such as *Fahrenheit 451* and *1984*, popular cultural figures like Robin Hood, Batman, and Judge Dredd, and the writings of Thomas Pyncheon and Harlan Ellison.

But whatever they do next, a crowd of people will be waiting. Because now, it seems, *everybody* has heard of the Wachowski brothers.

_ N O T E S _

Introduction
1. Richard Corliss, "Popular Metaphysics," *Time*, April 19, 1999, accessed at time.com

2. Richard Corliss, "Popular Metaphysics," *Time*, April 19, 1999, accessed at time.com

3. Richard Corliss, "Popular Metaphysics," *Time*, April 19, 1999, accessed at time.com

Chapter 1: Experience the Matrix
1. Richard Corliss, "Unlocking The Matrix," *Time*, May 12, 2003, accessed at time.com

2. "Sleeping Awake," P.O.D., © 2003 Famous Music Corp.

3. Accessed at www.relevantmagazine.com

Chapter 2: What Is the Matrix?
1. "Nothing Is Real: *The Matrix*," *The Chicago Reader*, accessed at www.chireader.com/movies/archives/1999/0499/04169.html

2. Greg's student, used by permission.

CHAPTER 3: POSTMODERN STEW
1. Richard Corliss, "Popular Metaphysics," *Time,* April 19, 1999, accessed at time.com

2. Joseph Campbell, with Bill Moyers, *The Power of Myth* (New York: Anchor, 1988), p. 152.

3. Christopher Vogler, *The Writer's Journey* (Studio City, Calif.: Michael Wise, 1998), p. 18.

4. Vogler, p. 24.

5. "Locked and Reloaded," *Premiere,* Jan. 2003, accessed at premiere.com

6. "Japan's anime master makes powerful films," *Christian Science Monitor,* October 29, 1999, accessed at csmonitor.com

7. Bill Moyers, "Of Myth and Men," *Time,* April 26, 1999, accessed at time.com

8. Richard Corliss, "Popular Metaphysics," *Time,* April 19, 1999, accessed at time.com

CHAPTER 4: ENLIGHTENED . . . FROM EAST TO WEST
1. Richard Corliss, "Popular Metaphysics," *Time,* April 19, 1999, accessed at time.com

2. Karen Armstrong, *A History of God* (New York: Knopf, 1993), p. 94.

3. Armstrong, pp. 95-96.

4. Armstrong, p. 96.

5. Mircea Eliade, *A History of Religious Ideas,* Vol. 2 (Chicago: University of Chicago Press, 1982), p. 372.

CHAPTER 5: PARADISE LOST
1. Genesis 11:6, *The Message.*

2. Douglas Adams, *The Hitchhiker's Guide to the Galaxy* (New York: Ballantine, 1995).

3. 2 Corinthians 12:3-4, *The Living Bible.*

4. Genesis 3:16, *The Message.*

CHAPTER 6: NEO: MY OWN PERSONAL JESUS
1. Matthew 10:34, *New International Version.*

CHAPTER 7: LEAP OF FAITH
1. Joshua 23:10, *The Message.*

2. Judges 7:3, *The Message.*

CHAPTER 8: REINVENTING MYTH FOR NEW GENERATIONS
1. Richard Corliss, "Popular Metaphysics," *Time,* April 19, 1999, accessed at time.com

2. Http://www.thestranger.com/1999-08-19/feature.html

3. "Of Myth and Men," *Time,* April 26, 1999, accessed at time.com

4. "Of Myth and Men," *Time,* April 26, 1999, accessed at time.com

5. Richard Corliss, "Popular Metaphysics," *Time,* April 19, 1999, accessed at time.com

6. Joseph Campbell, *Transformations of Myth Through Time* (New York: Harper&Row, 1990), p. 189.

7. Mircea Eliade, *A History of Religious Ideas,* Vol. 2 (Chicago: University of Chicago Press, 1982), pp. 186-187.

8. Eliade, p. 197.

CHAPTER 9: MORPHEUS: A VOICE CRYING IN THE WILDERNESS
1. Richard Corliss, "Popular Metaphysics," *Time*, April 19, 1999, accessed at time.com

2. *STARLOG* 261 (March 1999), accessed at http://www.starlog.com/tpages/morpheus_arc.htm.

3. Matthew 11:11.

4. Mircea Eliade, *A History of Religious Ideas*, Vol. 2 (Chicago: University of Chicago Press, 1982), p. 331.

5. Matthew 3:14, *The Message*.

6. *STARLOG* 261 (March 1999), accessed at http://www.starlog.com/tpages/morpheus_arc.htm.

7. *STARLOG* 261 (March 1999), accessed at http://www.starlog.com/tpages/morpheus_arc.htm.

8. *STARLOG* 261 (March 1999), accessed at http://www.starlog.com/tpages/morpheus_arc.htm.

CHAPTER 10: WAKE UP!
1. *A History of Religious Ideas*, Vol. 2 (Chicago: University of Chicago Press, 1982), p. 336.

2. Ephesians 5:13, *The Message*.

3. John 11:11.

4. Mark 13:35-37, *The Message*.

5. Mark 14:37-38,41, *The Message*.

6. Romans 13:11-12, *The Message*.

7. Elaine Pagels, *The Gnostic Gospels* (New York: Vintage, 1989), p. 126.

8. Isaiah 29:8, *The Message*.

9. Matthew 6:6, *The Message.*

CHAPTER 11: WALKING THE PATH

1. Richard Corliss, "Unlocking The Matrix," *Time*, May 12, 2003, accessed at time.com

2. Corliss.

3. Daniel 4:3, *The Message.*

CHAPTER 12: TRINITY: THE FEMALE FACE OF GOD

1. *A History of Religious Ideas,* Vol. 2 (Chicago: University of Chicago Press, 1982), p. 259.

2. Proverbs 8:20–22,35, *The Message.*

3. John 3:17.

4. Elaine Pagels, *The Gnostic Gospels* (New York: Vintage, 1989), p. 64.

5. Pagels, p. 57.

CHAPTER 13: I KNOW KUNG FU

1. *Gospel of Truth* 29:8–30:12.

2. Tony Jones, "Liberated by Reality," *Books & Culture,* Sept./Oct. 1999, accessed at christianitytoday.com

3. Richard Corliss, "Unlocking The Matrix," *Time*, May 12, 2003, accessed at time.com

4. John Carroll, *Constantine's Sword: The Church and the Jews* (Boston: Houghton Mifflin, 2001), p. 78.

5. Matthew 21:14, *The Message.*

6. Matthew 21:21, *The Message.*

7. Matthew 26:52-53, *The Message.*

CHAPTER 14: ENSLAVED TO CREATION
1. Matthew 6:24, *New International Version.*

2. Romans 1:1, *The Message.*

3. John 13:34.

4. John 15:13.

5. Mark 3:7-13, *The Message.*

6. Psalm 137:1, *The Message.*

7. Psalm 137:8-9, *The Message.*

8. Isaiah 28:16-17, *The Message.*

9. Isaiah 14:32, *The Message.*

10. John 8:34-36, *The Message.*

11. Greg's student, used by permission.

12. John 1:29, *New International Version.*

13. Psalm 2:7-12, *The Message.*

14. Jack Miles, *Christ: A Crisis in the Life of God* (New York: Vintage, 2002), p. 27.

15. Miles, p. 203.

CHAPTER 15: CYPHER: TEMPTER AND BETRAYER
1. "Nothing Is Real: *The Matrix*," *The Chicago Reader,* accessed at www.chireader.com/movies/archives/1999/0499/04169.html

2. Jack Miles, *Christ: A Crisis in the Life of God* (New York: Vintage, 2002), pp. 302-303.

3. Hosea 2:20, *The Message.*

4. Job 1:6, *The Message.*

5. John 12:5, *The Message.*

CHAPTER 16: IT COULD HAPPEN

1. Glenn Yeffeth, ed., *Taking the Red Pill* (Dallas, Tex.: BenBella Books, 2003), p. 199.

2. Acts 2:44.

3. Genesis 2:18.

4. Desmond Tutu, *The Rainbow People of God* (New York: Morrow, 1994), p. 93.

5. Yeffeth, p. 199.

6. Steve Silberman, "Matrix 2," *Wired,* May 2003: 116.

CHAPTER 17: APOCALYPSE NOW

1. Revelation 13:11–18, *The Message.*

2. Revelation 1:3, *The Message.*

3. Genesis 6:5–17, *The Message*

4. Bill Moyers, *Genesis: A Living Conversation* (New York: Doubleday, 1996), p. 132.

5. Revelation 14:1, *The Message.*

CONCLUSION

1. Matthew 21:21–22, *The Message.*

2. 2 Peter 1:10, *The Message.*

AFTERWORD FOR ARTISTS, STORYTELLERS, AND WRITERS
1. Joseph Campbell, with Bill Moyers, *The Power of Myth* (New York: Anchor, 1988), p. 2.

2. Campbell, p. 2.

3. Campbell, pp. 38–39.

4. James 2:14, *The Message*.

APPENDIX: ABOUT THE WACHOWSKI BROTHERS
1. Http://www.cleave.com/Sight/The_Matrix/wachowski.htm

2. Richard Corliss, "Unlocking the Matrix," *Time*, May 12, 2003, accessed at time.com

CHRIS SEAY is pastor of Ecclesia, a progressive Christian community in Houston, Texas, recognized for exploring spiritual questions of culture and breaking new ground in art, music, and film. He travels extensively speaking on faith and postmodernity. Seay, author of *The Gospel According to Tony Soprano*, *The Tao of Enron* (NavPress), and a contributor to *Stories of Emergence* and *The Slate Diaries*, has appeared on numerous radio and television broadcasts, including CNN and ABC News. His work has been reviewed in *USA Today*, *Entertainment Weekly*, and *Publishers Weekly*.

GREG GARRETT is the author of the Pulitzer Prize-nominated novel *Free Bird*, forty short stories, and numerous articles and essays on film, narrative, and spirituality. He directs Art & Soul, a nationally recognized festival of religion and the arts at Baylor University, where he is a professor of English. He lives in Austin, Texas.

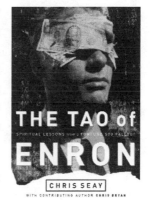